Due

JAN 2

VISUAL SCIENCE

COMPUTERS
AND MATHEMATICS

Carol Gourlay

Silver Burdett Company

Series Editor John Rowlstone
Editor John Liebmann
Design Richard Garratt
Picture Research Jenny Golden
Production John Moulder

First published 1982

Macdonald & Co. (Publishers) Ltd.
Holywell House
Worship Street
London EC2A 2EN

© Macdonald & Co. 1982

Adapted and Published in
the United States by
Silver Burdett Company,
Morristown, New Jersey

1982 Printing

ISBN 0-382-06662-6

Library of Congress
Catalog Card No. 82-50387

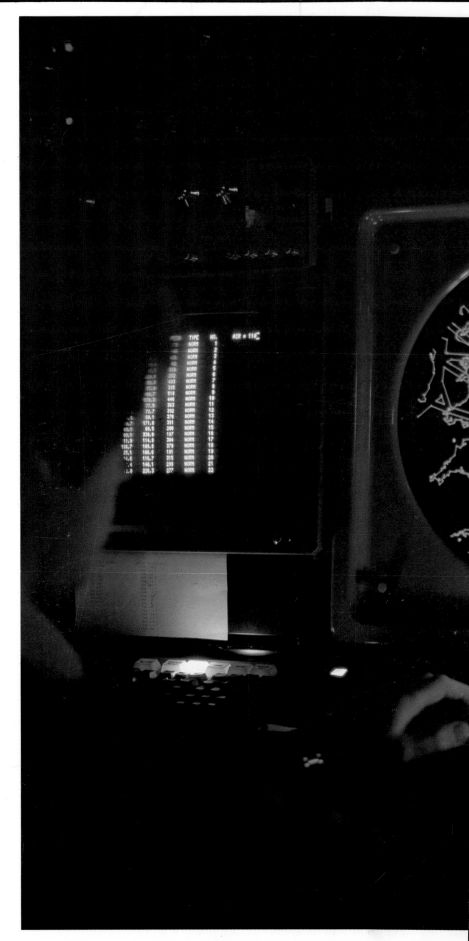

Right: The computerized display used
by British air-traffic controllers

Contents

Numbers and number system

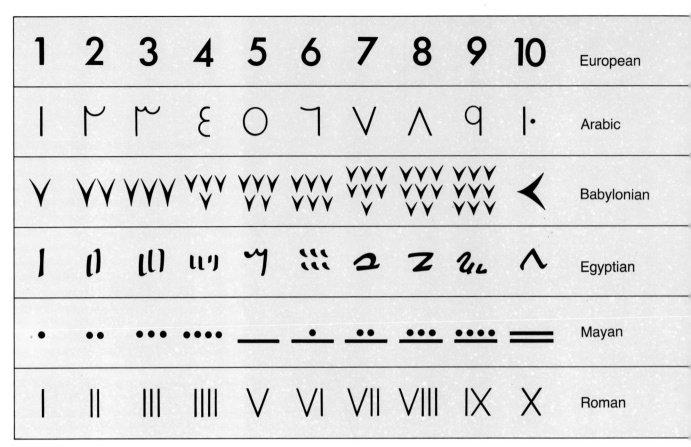

1	2	3	4	5	6	7	8	9	10	European

Arabic

Babylonian

Egyptian

Mayan

Roman

Above: Six different ways of writing the numbers 1-10. The European numerals (top) and the arabic numerals are two different ways of writing numbers in the same system, and both have a symbol to represent zero. Both are still in use today.

Below: Roman numerals often appear on clocks and watches; they are decorative rather than functional. For purely practical purposes, arabic numerals are easier to read.

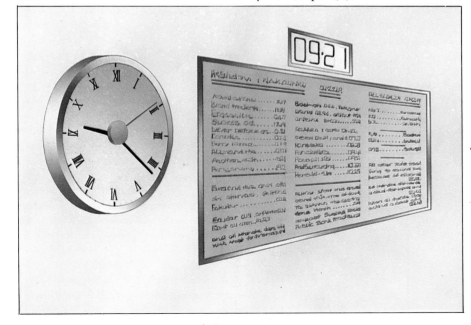

Just as an alphabet is a 'system' of letters, so there are also systems of numbers. These are sets of symbols which are used to write numbers. Different civilizations use different alphabets, and some have also used different number systems.

The ancient Greeks used the same symbols to represent both letters and numbers. The first letter of the alphabet, alpha (α), also stands for one,

the third letter, gamma (γ) stands for three, and so on.

Roman numerals

The number system invented by the Romans is still used occasionally. Like the Greeks, the Romans used letters to represent numbers. The number one is shown by the letter I. Other letters are V which corresponds to five, X which represents ten, L which represents fifty, C which stands for one hundred and M which represents one thousand.

Other numbers are made up from string of letters, starting with the one of highest value, which are added together. A letter coming *before* another one of higher value is *subtracted* from the total. So MM is 2000; MCM is 1900 MCMLXXX is 1980; and MCMLXXIX is 1979.

The importance of zero

Zero, or nought, was an important mathematical discovery. The big difference between the Greek and Roman number systems and our present-day system is that we use the number zero.

In our number system, the position of a symbol tells us its value. So 50 is ten times as large as 5; 500 is one hundred times as large; and 5000 is one thousand times as large. We use the

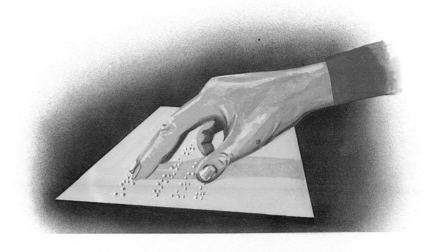

Right: A blind person reading by feeling a series of raised dots. This system, called Braille, is rather like the binary system: at any particular position, either the dot is present or it is absent. In writing binary numerals either the numeral is present in a particular position (shown by symbol '1') or absent (shown by the symbol '0').

number zero to show whether '5' means five ones, or five tens (fifty), or five hundreds, etc.

Number bases

We use ten symbols, or 'digits', to make up our modern numbers. We count things in bundles of tens, hundreds, thousands and so on. This method of counting in multiples of ten is called 'base 10' or 'decimal'. The name comes from the Latin word *decem* which means ten.

In our base-ten number system, the figures 10 stand for ten (1 = one bundle of ten; 0 = no units extra). If we used base eight, then the figures 10 would stand for eight (1 = one bundle of eight). In base eight we would write the number ten as 12 (1 = one bundle of eight; 2 = two extra units). Base eight is called the 'octal' system, and needs only eight symbols to group together to make numbers.

Computers work in the binary system, which uses base two. So in binary there are just two symbols, 0 and 1. Counting is done by making bundles of twos. The number of pages in this book, written in binary, is 110000. Even quite small numbers need a lot of digits when written in binary. One thousand in binary is 1111101000. This makes binary rather unsuitable for everyday use!

Digital computers work by recognizing the presence or absence of an electrical pulse, at a particular time. The 0 and 1 of the binary system correspond to the on–off flow of electricity in the computer's circuits.

Above right: Our number system and our money are both base-ten or 'decimal' systems. The metric weights and measures are also base-ten systems, but some of the older measures (such as feet and inches, or pounds and ounces) use other number bases. The metric system makes for easier calculations, especially in automatic weighing and pricing systems such as this one.

Right: The ancient Mesopotamians used sixty as the base of their number system.

Calculating aids

There are all sorts of devices that people use to help them count or do calculations. Some are very simple, and you might use them every day without realizing it. Others are complex and used only for special tasks.

All over the world, people use their fingers to count with. Fingers are the first mathematical aid that everyone learns to use. They are useful for doing simple addition and subtraction.

Faster than a calculator

One of the oldest mathematical aids is the abacus. It has been used for thousands of years. The first abacuses were just lines drawn in sand. People used small stones placed on the lines to represent numbers. They did the calculations by moving the stones.

The most common form of abacus used now consists of a frame with wooden or wire bars mounted on it. On each bar there are several beads which slide up and down. Numbers are shown by placing the beads in a particular position. Some abacuses have bars divided into two, with the beads on the upper parts representing five units.

Someone who is skilled at using an abacus can do long and complicated calculations on it faster than with an electronic calculator. Abacuses are still used a lot in shops, offices and even in banks in many parts of the world.

Ready reckoners

One very useful kind of mathematical aid is in the form of a set of tables, called ready reckoners. They are a short cut to

Top left: Fingers and thumbs make a useful mathematical aid.

Centre left: An abacus is still faster than an electronic calculator in the hands of a skilled user.

Bottom left: A simple calculator can be made with a few stones and some marks drawn on the ground. This one is being used to calculate 341 × 123. There are three plus four plus one stones along the top to represent 341. One plus two plus three stones down the side represent 123. The stones in each box represent the product of the numbers at the edges, above and to the side of it. So you put one stone (1 × 1) in the top right square. Four stones (4 × 1) go in the centre right square, etc. The answer to the calculation is found by adding the number of stones along each diagonal. It works out as 40943.

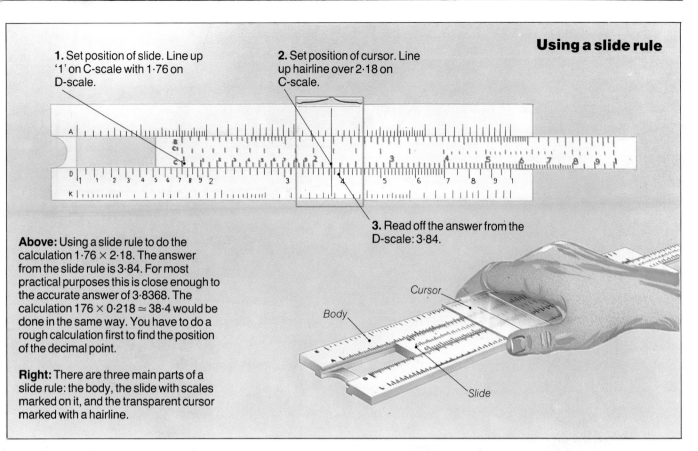

1. Set position of slide. Line up '1' on C-scale with 1·76 on D-scale.

2. Set position of cursor. Line up hairline over 2·18 on C-scale.

3. Read off the answer from the D-scale: 3·84.

Cursor

Body

Slide

Above: Using a slide rule to do the calculation 1·76 × 2·18. The answer from the slide rule is 3·84. For most practical purposes this is close enough to the accurate answer of 3·8368. The calculation 176 × 0·218 ≈ 38·4 would be done in the same way. You have to do a rough calculation first to find the position of the decimal point.

Right: There are three main parts of a slide rule: the body, the slide with scales marked on it, and the transparent cursor marked with a hairline.

the answers to a calculation – you don't actually have to do the sum, you just look up the answer in the ready reckoner.

There are special sets of ready reckoner tables for each calculation. For example, there are tables which show temperature in degrees Fahrenheit, with temperatures in Centigrade alongside. When a new decimal currency system was introduced in Britain in 1971 many people carried ready reckoners which showed prices in the old currency next to the same prices in new currency.

How to multiply by adding
Logarithms are a mathematical aid which allow you to do difficult multiplications and division just by adding two numbers together. There are special tables from which you can find the logarithm of any number. To multiply two numbers together, you look up the logarithm of each number in the table. Adding the two logarithms together gives the logarithm of the

answer. You can find the answer itself by using the tables again, but working backwards.

You can do divisions in a similar way: instead of dividing one number by the other you subtract the logarithm of one from the logarithm of the other to get the logarithm of the answer.

Slide rules work on a similar principle. They are very quick to use, and especially useful for doing approximate calculations. Even though electronic calculators are more accurate for large numbers, many engineers, scientists and designers have a slide rule handy on their desks. It is still cheaper than a calculator – and it doesn't need any batteries!

Right: Observatories are an ancient form of calculating aid. This one is at Jaipur in India, where the structures and instruments were used to calculate the positions of stars in the sky.

Introducing computers

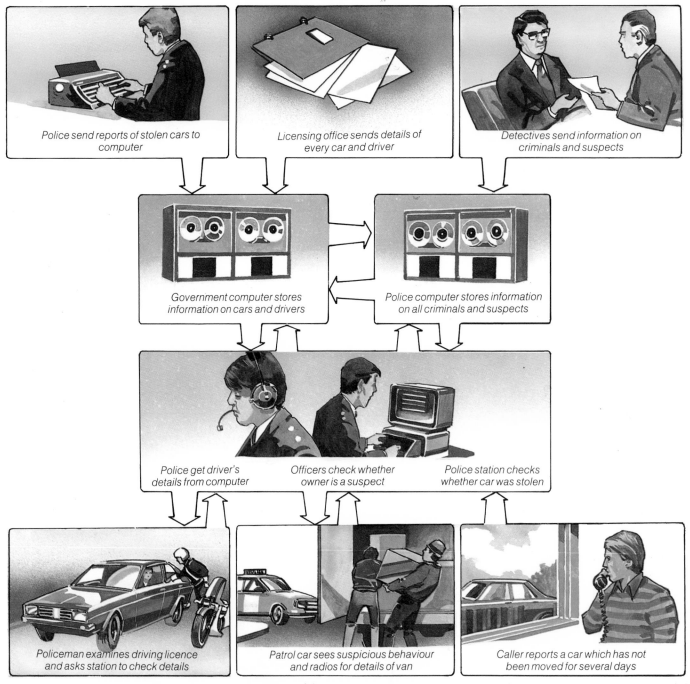

Police send reports of stolen cars to computer

Licensing office sends details of every car and driver

Detectives send information on criminals and suspects

Government computer stores information on cars and drivers

Police computer stores information on all criminals and suspects

Police get driver's details from computer

Officers check whether owner is a suspect

Police station checks whether car was stolen

Policeman examines driving licence and asks station to check details

Patrol car sees suspicious behaviour and radios for details of van

Caller reports a car which has not been moved for several days

Computers come in all sorts of sizes and do many different kinds of jobs. They range from tiny devices costing a few pence which do simple calculations, to complex machines which cost millions of dollars and can solve problems in minutes which no human could complete in a lifetime.

There are two quite different sorts of job which computers are good at. They can do calculations very fast and accurately. They can also store huge amounts of information and sort it out very quickly. Sometimes the same computer is used to do both jobs at the same time.

Huge machines

Development of electronic computers began during the Second World War. The United States Army wanted to calculate the trajectories of bombs and shells; to do it they ordered a machine called ENIAC – short for Electronic Numerical Integrator and Calculator. This huge machine, completed in 1946, contained 18,000 electronic valves, and used 150 kilowatts of electrical power. But despite its size it was very primitive. It was much slower than even a small modern computer, and could only do the special task allotted to it as it could not store programs.

Modern computers are so useful because they can do any calculation you want, according to a set of instructions called a program. The first programmable computer was built in 1949.

Soon afterwards manufacturers started selling computers which could be bought by any company that could afford them. The first of these, the Universal Automatic Computer (UNIVAC), appeared in the United States. For the first time it used magnetic tape for entering information, and it could recognise letters as well as numbers.

The first computer designed specially for business came from a Brit-

Left: A computer system designed to handle large quantities of information. The computers store millions of facts, and produce them again on demand. Without the computers, this would require a vast amount of paper and files, and an army of clerks to look after them. The computer allows the same amount of information to be stored more conveniently, and the information can be retrieved more quickly too.

Right: Automatic cameras actually have tiny computers built into them. In a split second they calculate the correct exposure to give a perfect picture every time. Engineers use computers to design the lenses, and the machines which make them are computer controlled.

ish firm of teashops called Lyons. With great foresight, Lyons produced the Lyons Electronic Office (LEO) in 1947 to help with the running of its business.

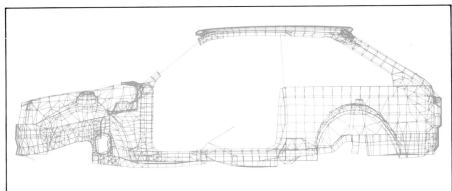

Cheap and powerful

Today there are hundreds of different types of computer. The valves of the earliest computers were soon replaced by transistors, which are much more reliable and use less electrical power. The transistors were in turn replaced by cheap integrated circuits or 'chips' in which an enormous number of components are packed into a tiny space.

Thanks to these technical advances there are today hundreds of different kinds of computer. You can now buy a computer which will fit into your pocket and has more calculating power than the ENIAC and UNIVAC put together.

The development of computers has been one of the most important events since the industrial revolution of the 18th century. They are already affecting the daily lives of most people all over the world.

Above right: Engineers and designers use computers more and more to help them with their work. Information from the designer's flat plans can be fed into the computer, which will then display a three-dimensional view on the screen.

Right: An early experimental computer called ACE which was built in 1950. The name stands for Automatic Computing Engine. The rows of little cylinders are electronic valves. In later computers these valves were replaced by transistors and then by integrated circuits or 'chips'.

Computer hardware

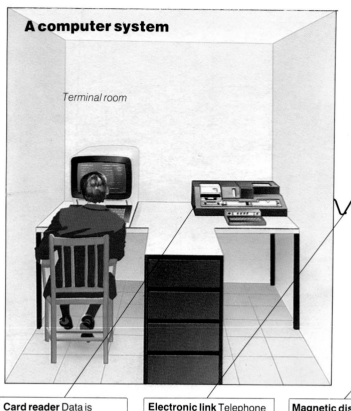

A computer system

Terminal room

Main computer room

Card reader Data is recorded as holes punched in cards; the reader converts them to electrical pulses.	**Electronic link** Telephone lines link the main computer room with distant terminals.	**Magnetic disc memory** Data is stored on discs which can be removed from the unit and stored.	**Line printer** Information is printed out at the rate of several complete lines each second.	**Magnetic tape memory** The tapes are similar to those in a tape recorder, they move much faster.

Like a motor car, a computer is made up of a set of parts which work together. In a small computer the parts are all contained inside the same box. In a large computer the various parts are always separate. They can be housed together in the same room or can be separated in different buildings, or even in different parts of the world.

The heart of a computer

At the heart of every computer is the central processing unit – usually called the CPU. This is the part of the computer where calculations are actually done. It does all its calculations using binary numbers. The CPU works very fast indeed, completing millions of calculations every second.

In order to work, every computer needs to be given a set of step-by-step instructions which tell it what to do.

Right: The central processing unit (CPU) controls the peripherals in the same way as a conductor controls the players in an orchestra. The CPU get information from input terminals and memories, and when it has finished its calculations it sends the results to a printer or VDU.

This set of instructions is called a program, and is stored in a memory inside the computer as a string of binary digits.

As well as storing the program, the memory stores the data which it uses in its calculations. For example, if the computer is programmed to calculate the weight of an aircraft it will need to know how many people are on board, how much their luggage weighs, etc.

All this is called the data. Like everything else it is stored in the computer in the form of binary digits.

The memory also stores the answers to calculations which have already been done. If only part of the calculation has been completed the CPU may need to use these answers later on. The central memory only stores the data which it needs immediately. It would quickly become cluttered if it stored all

Terminal room

VDU Data is entered by typing on the keyboard, and output is displayed as text on the screen.

CPU The part of the computer which does the calculations and controls the peripherals.

Cassette reader Data and programs are stored on an audio cassette. Information is printed out on paper.

Floppy disc memory Data and programs are stored on thin magnetic discs which are cheap and easy to use.

Teletype terminal Data is entered by typing on the keyboard, and information is printed out on paper.

the information it ever needed. Data or parts of the program which are only seldom needed are stored in extra memories, to be fed into the main memory when required.

Peripherals

In very small computers, these extra memories for storing data are inside the same box as the CPU. But most computers can add on separate memory units. There are several common types of memory unit, including magnetic tape, magnetic disc and floppy disc.

For the computer to be of any practical use you have to be able to get the data into it, and there has to be a way for the computer to tell you the results of its calculations. The peripheral units which feed information into the computer are called input terminals. They usually include a keyboard rather like a

typewriter keyboard.

Often the keyboard is connected straight to the computer. The keyboard or reader sends a series of electrical pulses into the machine. These are then converted into the binary digits which the computer understands.

Information comes out of the computer through an output unit. Usually this information is needed in written form. It can be printed out on a machine

like a fast electric typewriter. Where the information does not have to be kept, it can be displayed on a screen rather like a television screen called a visual display unit or VDU.

The peripherals are controlled by the CPU. It decides when to send information from one of the memories, when it needs data from one of the input terminals, and when it needs to display information on a particular VDU.

Right: The baseboard of a small computer in which all the parts are housed inside a single box. Each black rectangle contains a specialized 'chip'. One of them acts as the computer's CPU. Others control the output on the VDU screen and act as memories which store programs and data.

11

What's the betting?

Words like 'probably', 'likely' and 'possibly' mean that something might happen, but that it is not certain. There is a mathematical way of describing how likely it is that something will happen. This is called its probability.

Probability

If something is absolutely certain to happen it has a probability of 1. For example, the probability that you will die some day is 1. Anything which is certain *not* to happen has a probability of 0.

When an ordinary coin is tossed in the air a large number of times it will land with the head side up about the same number of times as it will land tail side up. On average, it will fall head side up once every two throws. So the probability of it showing heads is said to be $1 \div 2 = 0.5$.

When people bet, they try to calculate the probability of something happening. If there are sixteen football teams taking part in a competition, every one of them has a chance of winning. If they are all equally good, the probability that any one of them will win is $\frac{1}{16}$. But usually some of the teams are better than the others. Bookmakers guess at the probability when they fix the betting odds. For the favourite in the competition, they might fix the odds at 3 to 1 against. This means that they think the team has three chances of losing to every chance it has of winning, or that it will win once in every four games, on average.

At random

Suppose you wanted to find out how most people in your area travel to work. Of course you could ask everybody, but that might mean talking to tens of thousands of people. So you would have to ask just a few people, and hope that they were typical of the rest. This is called taking a sample. A sample which is typical of a larger population is called a random sample.

Finding a truly random sample can be surprisingly difficult. Standing in the road and asking everyone who went by would not be good enough because you would miss anyone travelling by car or bus. Even if you include them, what about people travelling by train? Great care must be taken to make sure that samples are not biased in this way.

Statistics

Numerical information can be collected from random samples, or from a series of related events such as the results of

Above: Roulette is a game of pure chance. There is an equal probability that the ball will end up in any one of the numbers on the wheel.

Above: The probability of a coin coming down 'heads' is exactly 0·5. On average one throw in every two will be 'heads'.

Above: What's the chance of getting on the bus? The probability is low at times when the bus is full. It is lowest of all for the people waiting at the back of the queue.

Above: Winning tickets in a lottery are chosen at random to make sure that each one has an equal chance. The tickets must be thoroughly mixed.

Right: A barrier being built across the Thames near London to prevent floods. Experts say that the probability of flooding is about 0·1 in any one year. It is not certain that the river will ever flood, but the probability is high enough to make the cost of building the barrier worthwhile.

football matches. When this information is collected together it is called the statistics about the subject concerned.

Statistics must always be interpreted carefully. For example, accident statistics show that most car accidents happen near the driver's home. This could mean that people are particularly careless when they are driving in their own neighbourhood. Or it could mean that most journeys are short, so drivers are usually close to home. More statistics about people's driving habits would be needed to find the true reason.

Above: A gardener sowing a row of seeds knows that not all of them will germinate. If the probability of germinating is low, extra seeds must be sown.

Above: In card games, players gamble on getting the right combination of cards. By estimating the probability of getting the right card, players improve their chances.

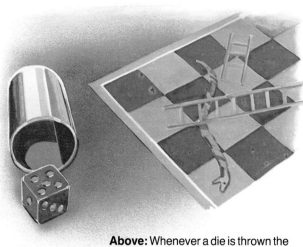

Above: Bookmakers estimate the probability of each horse winning its race in order to calculate the betting odds. Short odds mean a high probability of winning.

Above: Whenever a die is thrown the probability of the number a player wants is always one chance in six or ⅙. With more than one die the probability is increased.

One step at a time

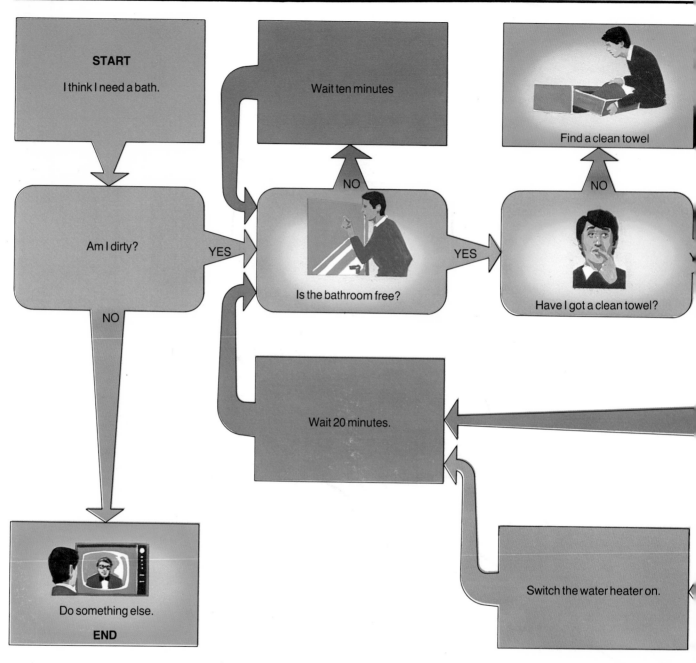

START

I think I need a bath.

Am I dirty?

YES

NO

Wait ten minutes

Is the bathroom free?

NO

YES

Find a clean towel

Have I got a clean towel?

NO

Wait 20 minutes.

Switch the water heater on.

Do something else.

END

Logic is a way of approaching problems step by step. Very complex problems can be solved using logic by breaking them down into simple steps, so long as the outcome of each step is known.

Games and logic

Snakes and ladders is a game of pure chance. Logic does not help to predict the outcome of the game. It all depends on how the dice fall. But chance plays no part in some other games such as chess and draughts. The rules allow each player to make certain moves. The result of the game depends only on which of those moves each player chooses to make.

A good player thinks something like

this: 'If I make *this* move, then my opponent will be able to make *that* or *that* move. That will leave me in a better position and I will be able to . . .' and so on. The further ahead the player can think, the better he or she will be at playing the game.

Computers and logic

A computer works logically. It solves problems by breaking them down into very simple steps. It then works through the problem step by step until it gets to the answer.

Computers are good at playing logical games. They never forget the rules they have to work by, since they are stored in the program. A computer

can be programmed to learn as it goes along. It does this by remembering every move its human opponent plays. Before making a move of its own, it tries to find out if it has been faced with a similar position before. If it has, it looks at what its opponent did the last time, and so it learns its opponent's strategy. Such programmes are very hard to beat.

Flow charts

All complex problems or processes can be broken down into simple parts. A diagram which shows a problem broken down in this way is called a flow chart. Using a series of boxes and arrows, it leads through a sequence of

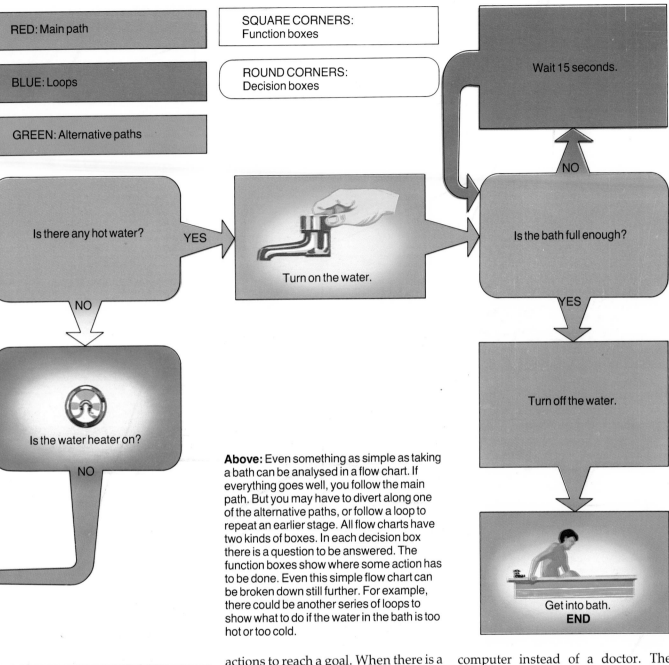

RED: Main path

BLUE: Loops

GREEN: Alternative paths

SQUARE CORNERS: Function boxes

ROUND CORNERS: Decision boxes

Is there any hot water? — YES → Turn on the water. → Is the bath full enough?

NO ↓

Is the water heater on?

NO

Wait 15 seconds.

NO ↑ Is the bath full enough?

YES ↓

Turn off the water.

Get into bath.
END

Above: Even something as simple as taking a bath can be analysed in a flow chart. If everything goes well, you follow the main path. But you may have to divert along one of the alternative paths, or follow a loop to repeat an earlier stage. All flow charts have two kinds of boxes. In each decision box there is a question to be answered. The function boxes show where some action has to be done. Even this simple flow chart can be broken down still further. For example, there could be another series of loops to show what to do if the water in the bath is too hot or too cold.

actions to reach a goal. When there is a question, it must always have a yes or no answer. Different answers lead into different branches of the chart. Flow charts can be drawn to illustrate any sequence or any problem. They can show how to solve a mathematical equation, or just what you have to do when you run a bath or buy a tee-shirt.

Doctors use computers to help them find out what is wrong with a patient. The patient can be interviewed by a

Left: Noughts and crosses is a game of logic. One obvious logical rule is that you must always add an X to complete a row if two Xs are already there, as that is the way that the Xs win the game.

computer instead of a doctor. The computer displays questions on a VDU, and the patient answers 'Yes' or 'No'. The computer chooses its questions depending on the answers the patient gives. For example, if the computer asks 'Do you sleep well at night?' and the patient replies 'No', the computer will ask more questions about sleeping. If the patient answers 'Yes', the computer goes on to another topic.

Of course, nobody expects that these diagnostic computers will replace doctors. They cannot provide the human understanding which a good doctor has. But they are useful for doing routine, time-consuming interviews for the doctor.

15

Software and programming

AT THE COMPUTER...

TELL ME WHO DR. SMITHS PATIENTS ARE!!!

LATER...

BASIC PROGRAM

A computer system is made up of dead electronic components. It cannot think for itself, and has to be told exactly what to do. However fast a computer can work, however big its memory, it is useless unless it has been given instructions about the job it is to do.

Programs and software
The instructions are called programs, and telling a computer what to do and how to do it is called programming. The programs which are used by a computer are called software (while the machinery itself is called the hardware).

There are two kinds of software. Every computer needs a set of instructions which tell it how to operate itself and all the attached peripherals. This is the system software. Without it the

computer is helpless. Computer manufacturers usually write the programs that make up the system software and install them permanently in the computer's internal memory.

Application software is the name for programs which are loaded into a computer to tell it how to do a specific job.

Programming languages
The computer works in binary code, so the program must be in binary too. Writing out long programs in binary 0s and 1s would be terribly slow, as programs often contain thousands of instructions. So special programming languages have been developed to provide the computer programmer with a short cut.

The operator feeds instructions into

Above: A programming language such as BASIC enables the programmer to communicate with the computer in a language they both understand.

Right: Writing a computer program is like planning a journey. There are many choice to be made, and the most obvious route is not necessarily the best.

the computer in the programming language. The computer itself the translates them into binary code. Th instructions for doing this are part o the computer's system software.

One of the most popular languages BASIC. It can be used for any kind o program, and most small compute use a version of BASIC. Like mo: programming languages it is easier t learn than a foreign language as it ha very few words.

Debugging
After a program for a particular job ha been written, the next step is to test out. It is very rare for a program to wor first time. An error nearly alway creeps in somewhere. Finding th error and correcting it is called debug ging.

Sometimes the program will wor properly for a while until somethin crops up which the programmer forgo to allow for. New 'bugs' can emerg even after a program has been runnin for years.

Left: A journalist typing his story into a computer terminal. The computer combine several journalists' work and controls the machinery which sets the stories in type. Programs for complex systems like this must be written very carefully, otherwise an unexpected event will bring everything grinding to a halt.

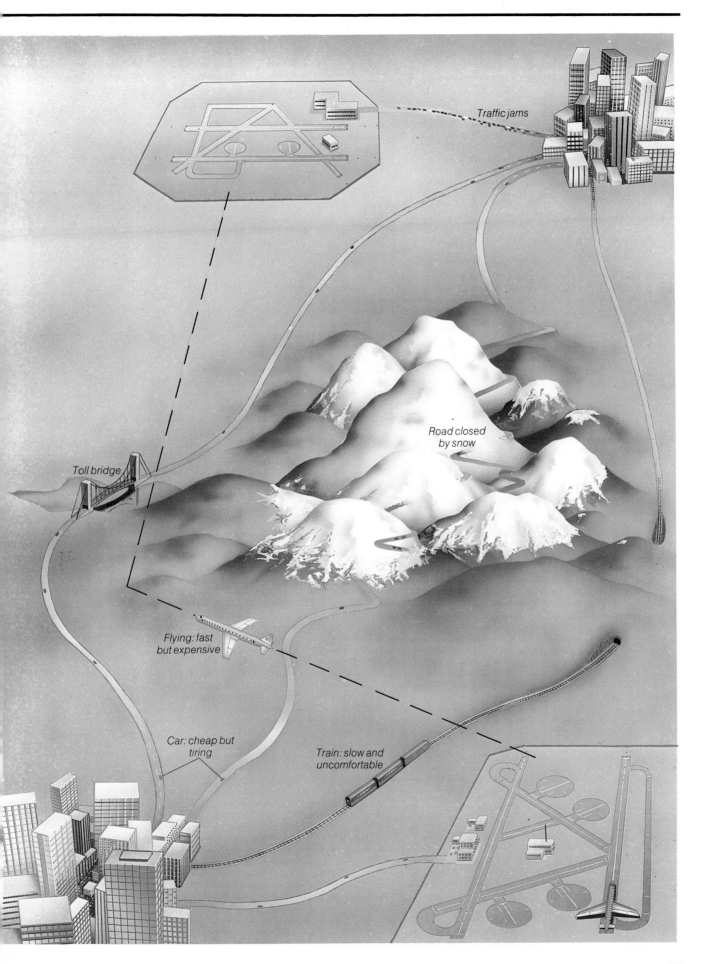

Traffic jams

Road closed
by snow

Toll bridge

Flying: fast
but expensive

Car: cheap but
tiring

Train: slow and
uncomfortable

Talking to computers

Right: The keyboard of a modern computer terminal lets the operator enter data and programs straight into the machine. It is usually connected to a VDU screen which displays the data as it is being keyed. The operator can therefore check that it has been typed properly, and correct any mistakes before the computer does its calculations. A small, blinking light called a cursor shows where the computer will place the next character to be keyed in. When making a correction the cursor is placed underneath the incorrect symbol before the correction is inserted.

The function keys are used for specialized purposes such as going back over a line to rewrite it, deleting mistakes or scrolling the text – making it roll up or down the screen.

The numeral keys are set together in a numeric pad. The pattern of the numbers is always the same as the pattern used for the keyboard of an ordinary calculator.

The alphabet keys are arranged like the keys on an ordinary typewriter. This is sometimes called the QWERTY arrangement after the order of the first six keys in the top row.

The operator uses these keys to position the cursor. It can be moved in any direction, and there is a 'cursor home' key which sends it back to the top left-hand corner of the display.

Computers and computer operators both understand programming languages. But computers do not have eyes or ears. Unless they are attached to special equipment they cannot read a set of instructions typed or written out on a piece of paper. So some method has to be found for entering instructions and data into the computer.

Punched cards

The cheapest method of putting data into a computer is also the oldest. Punched cards have been used for controlling machinery since the early days of the Industrial Revolution. They were used to vary the pattern of cloth produced by automatic weaving looms.

The cards used for computers are punched with a series of two or three holes for each character. A single card usually has space for 80 or 90 characters, which is enough for most simple instructions. A complete program is made up of a pack of cards – one card for each instruction. One advantage of using punched cards is that a program can be corrected or changed simply by inserting new cards into the pack and removing the unwanted ones.

Direct entry

On modern computers, instructions and data are entered by typing them out on a keyboard which is attached directly to the computer. This is called direct data entry. The keyboard has a series of alphabet keys, arranged as on a typewriter. There are also keys for numerals, and special function keys which give instructions to the computer telling it what to do with the data it has just received.

The terminal usually includes a VDU screen. The data appears on the screen as it is tapped out on the keys. A computer can be programmed to check the data as it is entered. For example, it can check that an address includes a postal code. If it finds something wrong, it will flash a message on the screen.

Above: A punched card of the type used for computers (shown approximately two-thirds life size). Each letter or number is represented by a code of one or two holes. For example, the number '4' is shown by a hole punched in line 4; the letter 'U' is shown by two holes, one in line 4 and one in line 0. Using a card-punch machine, the rectangular holes are automatically punched in the correct place as the operator taps out instructions or data on a keyboard. At the same time it types out the corresponding symbol along the top of the card. When a whole set of cards is ready they are fed through a 'reader' which scans each card column by column. It sends an electrical pulse to the computer for each hole that it detects. The reader can scan several cards every second, so a large amount of data can be entered quite quickly.

OCR and bar coding

A computer can be programmed to recognise specially formed marks. This is called optical character recognition (OCR). In this way data can be fed to the computer automatically, without an operator having to key it in.

Most supermarket goods are now marked with a row of little black and white stripes. These make up a bar code. The pattern of the stripes corresponds to a particular code number. Every product is given its own code number. Some supermarkets have installed special equipment at the checkouts which recognises bar codes.

This information is sent back to the computer, which displays a description of the product and its price on a small screen at the checkout. The computer adds up the cost of each customer's purchases. At the same time it keeps a check of how much of each line has been sold. The store manager can find out from the computer which products are selling well, and the computer itself can automatically order new stock to keep the shelves filled.

Engineers are trying to develop machines that will read handwriting. At present, it is only possible to read very carefully formed characters. Some hand-written marks can already be

read by computer devices, by a process called optical mark recognition. The computer detects the absence or presence of a mark on the paper at a particular point. Multiple-choice examination papers, where the candidate places a mark to indicate the answer, are read by OMR devices.

Above: This supermarket checkout desk has no cash register. A computer reads the bar codes marked on the goods, records each sale and adds up the customer's bill.

Below: The operator can 'draw' directly onto a VDU screen. Special programs detect the position of the pen, and illuminate the screen at that point.

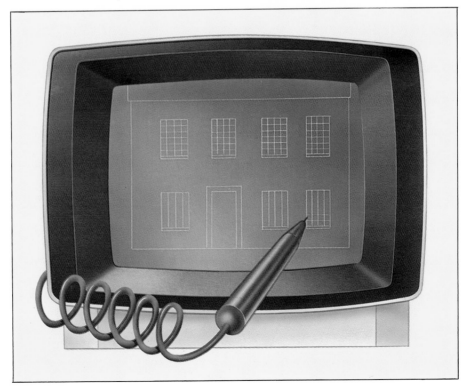

Storing information

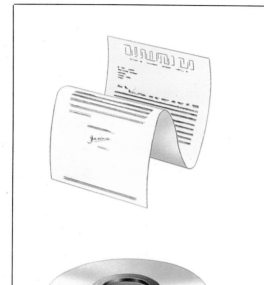

About 2,500 ordinary business letters can be stored on a single disc.

The text of this book could be stored on a single disc about 60 times over.

Ten 10,000-word novels can be stored on a single disc.

Information that is to be processed by a computer needs to be stored in three places. It must be stored somewhere inside the CPU where it will be processed. It needs to be stored somewhere outside the CPU but still easily accessible to the computer. It also needs to be stored somewhere away from the computer when it is not needed immediately.

ROM and RAM

The computer's internal memory will store small pieces of data that it is working on. This memory does not have to be particularly large, but it does have to work very quickly so that the working of the computer is not delayed while it sends items of information to and from the memory. In modern computers these memories are in the form of tiny electrical circuits engraved on silicon 'chips'. To expand a computer's memory, extra chips are installed.

There are two kinds of internal memory called ROM and RAM. ROM

Left: A magnetic core memory unit. Early computers used stacks of these units to form their random-access memories. Each ring can be magnetized in two different ways by passing a current through the wires. Modern memory chips work on the same principle, but are much smaller.

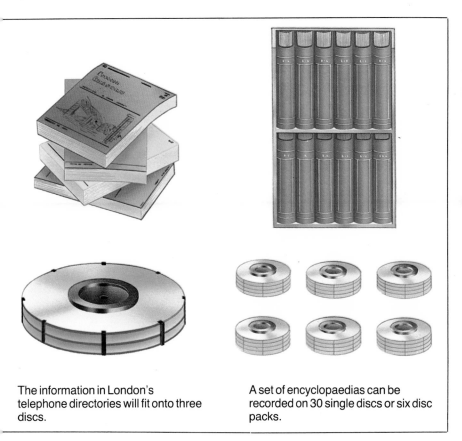

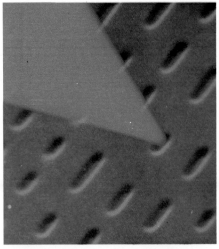

The information in London's telephone directories will fit onto three discs.

A set of encyclopaedias can be recorded on 30 single discs or six disc packs.

Above: The surface of a videodisc, magnified over 1000 times. Information is recorded permanently by means of tiny holes etched in the surface of the disc. It is detected by a fine beam of light from a laser.

Left: Magnetic discs can store large quantities of information. A single disc holds a million characters or more. As disc technology advances, even greater amounts of data will be crammed onto smaller discs.

stands for read-only memory, and it stores all the vital instruction programs. If these instructions were lost, the computer could not work. The contents of ROM cannot be erased and new instructions cannot be added – hence the name. The RAM (random access memory) can be used over and over again. Like magnetic tape, you can record and erase as you wish.

External memories

Outside the computer, the most common way of storing information is on magnetic discs and tapes. Information is recorded and read by a special 'head' as the tape moves past.

Magnetic discs are coated with magnetic oxide, and data is recorded on them in concentric tracks. As the disc revolves, the head can move in and out very fast, so it can reach any part of the disc in a very short time.

The smallest computers use floppy discs. These are flexible, and only 12 to 20 centimetres in diameter. They are

kept inside a protective paper case, with a hole in one side for the read-write head to enter.

Large computers use rigid magnetic discs, each of which can hold millions of characters. They often come in packs of several discs, mounted one on top of the other with the read-write heads in between. The heads float over the surface of the disc and do not come into contact with it at all.

Back-up storage

It is usual to copy all the information held in the main memories. The back-up copies are then stored in secure, fire-proof vaults or safes. This is done to make sure that essential information cannot be lost for good. A company could lose all its orders, a hospital all its records, if its computer were damaged. Tape is often used for back-up storage because it is cheap.

Right: Scale diagram showing the read-write head of a rigid magnetic disc. The distance between the head and the disc is so small that even a dust particle could cause it to crash onto the surface. The discs must therefore be kept in a perfectly clean atmosphere to prevent this.

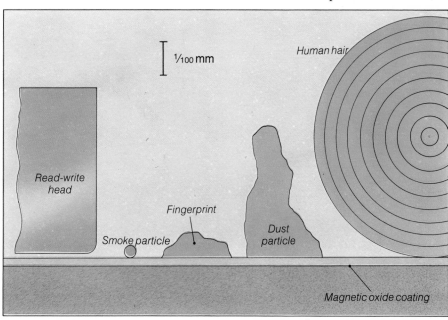

Printout

Above: A videotex subscriber uses a special keypad to display the information she wants on her television screen. Videotex (called Prestel in Britain) draws on a huge database stored on a network of small computers.

After the computer has completed its calculations it must have a way of sending the information to the person who wants to use it. This might be a specialist computer operator, a company's sales department, a customer or a member of the public. The form in which the information is presented can be chosen to suit the user's particular needs.

VDU displays

One of the easiest and cheapest ways of presenting processed information is on a VDU screen. Information can be called up and displayed almost instantaneously. It is specially useful when information is required from moment to moment but does not have to be recorded permanently. Some small computers do not even need a specialized VDU display, but are plugged into an ordinary television set instead.

The characters on a VDU screen are made up from dots of light grouped together. Usually the letters appear white on a black background, but some users prefer black on a white background. Green on black is another popular combination. Computers can be programmed to display full colour on a colour VDU. This is particularly useful for graphs and charts. Some VDUs with a small computer built into them can do simple calculations away from the main computer. They are called 'intelligent' terminals.

Hard copy

For many purposes the computer's user wants its output in a form which can be kept. This means that it can be used for reference later, or sent to other people who want to see it. A computer output printed on paper is called 'hard copy'.

Impact printers are the most common variety of hard copy output units. They print by hitting an inked ribbon with the form of the character, just like an ordinary typewriter. Golf ball and daisy wheel machines are useful because they can print much faster than a typewriter.

Dot matrix printers form the character from a block, or matrix, of dots. They do not print such clear characters as other impact printers, but they are much faster and can also draw diagrams and simple pictures.

One drawback of all impact printers is that they are rather noisy. The

Below: A bank statement printed out by a computer. The bank can program its computer to issue a statement at regular intervals. It automatically prints out the information which the customer needs, and even includes the address.

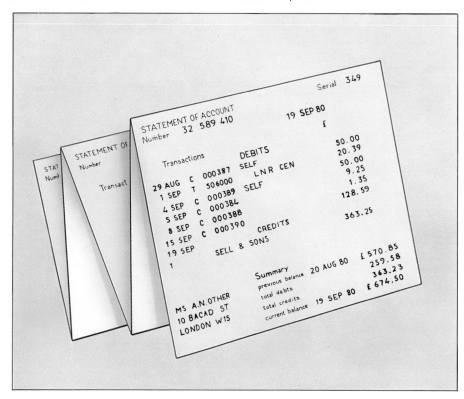

```
US ASCII:
 !"#$%&'()*+,-./0123456789:;<=>?@ABCDEFGHIJKLMNOPQRSTUVWXYZ[\]^_`abcdefghijklmnopqrstuvwxyz{|}~
Swedish I:
 !"#$%&'()*+,-./0123456789:;<=>?@ABCDEFGHIJKLMNOPQRSTUVWXYZÄÖÅ^_`abcdefghijklmnopqrstuvwxyzäöå~
Swedish II/Finnish:
 !"#$%&'()*+,-./0123456789:;<=>?£ABCDEFGHIJKLMNOPQRSTUVWXYZÄÖÅÜ_éabcdefghijklmnopqrstuvwxyzäöåü
Danish/Norwegian:
 !"#$%&'()*+,-./0123456789:;<=>?£ABCDEFGHIJKLMNOPQRSTUVWXYZÆØÅÜ_éabcdefghijklmnopqrstuvwxyzæøåü
German:
 !"#$%&'()*+,-./0123456789:;<=>?§ABCDEFGHIJKLMNOPQRSTUVWXYZÄÖÜ^_`abcdefghijklmnopqrstuvwxyzäöüß
British:
 !"£$%&'()*+,-./0123456789:;<=>?@ABCDEFGHIJKLMNOPQRSTUVWXYZ[\]^_`abcdefghijklmnopqrstuvwxyz{|}‾
Dutch:
 !"£$%&'()*+,-./0123456789:;<=>?@ABCDEFGHIJKLMNOPQRSTUVWXYZ[\]^_`abcdefghijklmnopqrstuvwxyz{|}~
Italian:
 !"£$%&'()*+,-./0123456789:;<=>?§ABCDEFGHIJKLMNOPQRSTUVWXYZ°çé^_ùabcdefghijklmnopqrstuvwxyzàòèì
French/Belgian:
 !"£$%&'()*+,-./0123456789:;<=>?àABCDEFGHIJKLMNOPQRSTUVWXYZ°ç§^_`abcdefghijklmnopqrstuvwxyzéùè¨
Spanish:
 !"£$%&'()*+,-./0123456789:;<=>?§ABCDEFGHIJKLMNOPQRSTUVWXYZiñ¿^_`abcdefghijklmnopqrstuvwxyz°ñç~
Japanese:
 !"#$%&'()*+,-./0123456789:;<=>?@ABCDEFGHIJKLMNOPQRSTUVWXYZ[¥]^_`abcdefghijklmnopqrstuvwxyz{|}‾
```

Above: The output from a matrix printer. It can be programmed to produce an enormous variety of different characters, or even diagrams. But the characters look rather fuzzy, and when they are magnified you can see that each one is made up of a pattern of dots.

Right: Golf ball and daisy wheel elements are used on impact printers to print solid characters. They print very clearly, but only a limited number of characters are available on each element. On a golf ball the letters are on the surface of the ball. On a daisy wheel they are on the end of each spoke.

thermal printer is a quieter type. It produces characters from a matrix on heat-sensitive paper. Electrographic and electrostatic printers also require specially treated paper. Electrographic printers use paper that is sensitive to light, while the electrostatic type needs paper that reacts to an electric charge.

Ink-jet printers work by squirting droplets of ink at the paper. The ink is deflected electronically to form the required character. Ink-jet printers can be programmed to form a wide range of different characters, and in theory can even reproduce signatures.

Visual information

Many kinds of information are presented in the form of numbers. When this information has to be taken in at a glance, the numbers can be converted into visual or pictorial form. This makes the information easier to understand.

Graphs, pictograms and pie charts are all ways of presenting information visually. Each method has its own advantages and disadvantages. Pictograms are very simple and direct, but do not convey much information. Graphs are very precise, but they are not as striking visually.

Graphs and charts can be misleading if they are not examined carefully. Some graphs are intentionally misleading – suggesting that a particular product is much better than it really is, for example.

Pie charts

Suppose that 30 people eating at a restaurant order the following dishes:

Roast chicken: 10 people
Fish and chips: 8 people
Spaghetti: 7 people
Hamburgers: 4 people
Curry: 1 person

This information can be displayed on a diagram, called a pie chart, consisting of a circle divided into segments. The entire circle is 360 degrees, and there are 30 people, so each person's choice takes up $360 \div 30 = 12$ degrees.

Each dish is represented by one segment of the pie chart. One person chose curry, so the segment for curry is $12°$; four people chose hamburgers so that section takes up $4 \times 12° = 48°$. The pie chart is ideal for showing proportions. For example you can see at a glance that exactly half the people chose either fish or spaghetti.

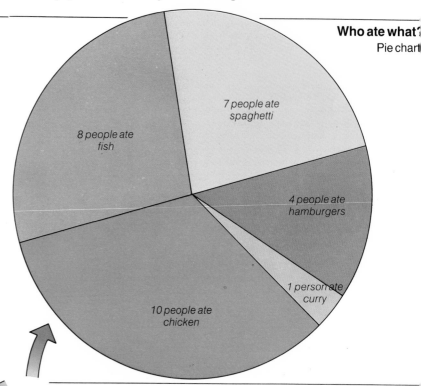

Who ate what?
Pie chart

7 people ate spaghetti

8 people ate fish

4 people ate hamburgers

1 person ate curry

10 people ate chicken

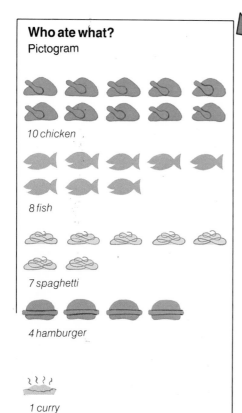

Who ate what?
Pictogram

10 chicken

8 fish

7 spaghetti

4 hamburger

1 curry

Pictograms

The same information can be presented in more than one way. The choices made by the people at the restaurant can be shown simply by putting one symbol for every meal. Each symbol looks like the dish that it represents, so that it is obvious at a glance how many people ate which dish. A diagram like this is called a pictogram.

Larger numbers can also be represented by pictograms. Suppose the number of cars using a city car park

each day was as follows:

Monday 570
Tuesday 520
Wednesday 530
Thursday 510
Friday 620
Saturday 320
Sunday 150

It would be impractical to show one symbol for every car, so there is one symbol for every 100 cars. Parts of 100 are shown by portions of a symbol.

Histograms and graphs

A histogram (also called a bar chart) consists of a series of columns or bars. The height of each column depends on the size of the quantity it represents. A particular shop counts the number of overcoats it sells each month for a year. The sales figures are shown on the histogram below.

A weather station in the same town keeps records of the average temperatures on the first day of each month. These figures are plotted on the graph below. After the points are plotted they can be connected together by a smooth line. This allows the average temperature at any time of the year to be read off from the graph. For example, the average temperature for the middle of October is about 12°·

With the graph and histogram placed side by side it is easy to see that most coats were sold in the coldest months, and least in the hottest. There is a correlation between temperature and the sales of coats.

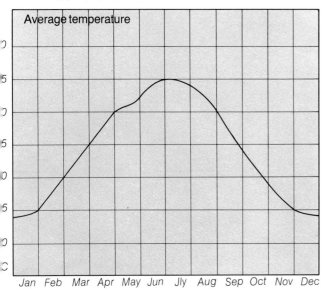

Average temperature

Jan Feb Mar Apr May Jun Jly Aug Sep Oct Nov Dec

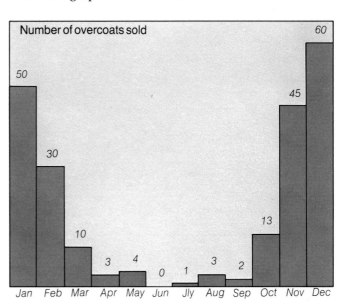

Number of overcoats sold

60 50 45 30 13 10 3 4 0 1 3 2

Jan Feb Mar Apr May Jun Jly Aug Sep Oct Nov Dec

How many cars?

Monday	570
Tuesday	520
Wednesday	530
Thursday	510
Friday	620
Saturday	320
Sunday	150

Below: The seven tugs, all pulling in different directions, combine to tow the oil platform. The different towing forces of the tugs can be represented visually on a vector diagram. The diagram can then be used to find the size of the towing force on the oil platform, and the exact direction in which it will move.

Like and unlike

It is often useful to be able to classify things into groups whose members have some important feature in common. For example, when planning activities at a sports centre you could divide people into groups according to the sports they would like to play.

The mathematical name for groups like these is a 'set'. Each set can be given a name:

{people who want to play
five-a-side football} = P
{people who want to play
badminton} = Q
{people who want to play
squash} = R
{people who want to swim} = S

All these people have something else in common: they all go to the sports centre. So there is another set:

{everyone who goes to the sports
centre} = E

This is called the universal set, because it includes everyone in the problem we are thinking about.

Absolutely anything can be classified as part of a set. Objects, people, even ideas, can be divided into sets. The sets and the universal set can be chosen to suit any particular problem. A head teacher could divide the children in a school into the following sets:

{all the boys}
{all the girls}
{first-year children}
{children under 1·20 metres tall}

For the head teacher, all the children in the school make up the universal set.

For a librarian, the universal set might be all the books in the library. They could be divided into fiction, non-fiction, hardback, paperback, children's books, reference books, etc.

Right: This photograph, which was taken in an airport terminal, shows about 25 people. Every one of the people is different: some are men, some are women; some have luggage, others do not; some are wearing jackets, etc. In the smaller diagrams on this page they are divided into various different sets. For this purpose, the 25 people in the picture make up the universal set.

Above: The universal set of all the people in the picture can be divided into smaller sets:

A = {people on the balcony}
B = {people on the main floor}
C = {people sitting down}

Every person in the universal set is a member of at least one of these sets. Some of the people are members of more than one set. All the people sitting down (set C) are on the main floor, so they are also members of set B. Set C is called a 'subset' of set B because all its members are also members of set B. This can be written:

C ∈ B

Left: D is the set of people who are near the stairs. In the main picture you can see that there are seven people in set D: two upstairs and five downstairs. Those five make up a set of their own – set E. E is a subset of both D and B, and is called the 'intersection' of D and B. This is written: E = D ∩ B.

Right: The set F is made up of people who are near the stairs, together with the people on the balcony. Both A and D are subsets of F, which is called the 'union' of A and D. This can be written: F = A ∪ D.

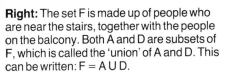

The way the money goes

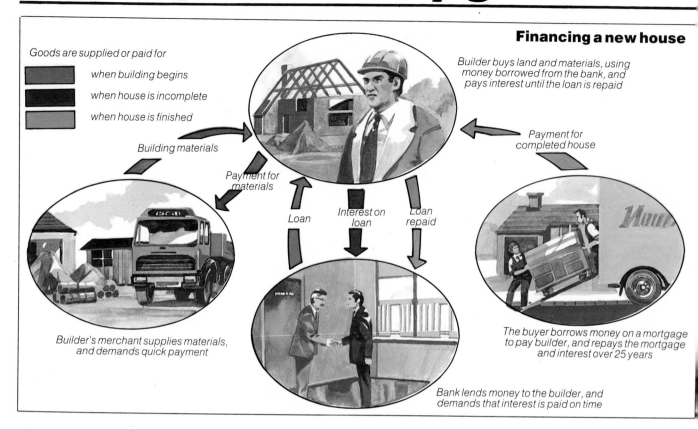

Financing a new house

Goods are supplied or paid for

- █ when building begins
- █ when house is incomplete
- █ when house is finished

Building materials

Payment for materials

Builder's merchant supplies materials, and demands quick payment

Loan

Interest on loan

Loan repaid

Builder buys land and materials, using money borrowed from the bank, and pays interest until the loan is repaid

Payment for completed house

The buyer borrows money on a mortgage to pay builder, and repays the mortgage and interest over 25 years

Bank lends money to the builder, and demands that interest is paid on time

---

Business and commerce rely on mathematics. The main aim of most businesses is to make a profit. Every firm needs to keep a constant check on what it spends and the money it receives.

Percentages

The calculation of a percentage is at the centre of many commercial agreements and procedures. A percentage is an amount expressed as a portion of one hundred.

To turn a fraction into a percentage, you simply divide the bottom number into the top number, and multiply the result by 100. Suppose that 232 households out of 800 own telephones. The percentage of these households which own telephones is $(232 \div 800) \times 100 = 29$ per cent.

Percentages are used in the lending and borrowing of money. People deposit money with banks, and the bank then lends this money to other customers. The bank charges the borrower a certain amount of money. It also pays something to the person who deposited the money in the first place. These sums of money are called interest.

Interest is usually calculated as a percentage of the amount of money borrowed or lent, to be paid each year.

Simple interest is paid as a fixed percentage of the loan. The amount of interest remains the same every time interest is paid.

Credit

Buying goods 'on credit' is a way of borrowing money. Shops will allow customers to pay for expensive goods over a period of time, but they will charge interest on the price of the purchase. When people buy a house, they usually have to borrow some money from a bank or building society to help pay for it. A loan to buy a house is called a mortgage.

Many people prefer to pay for goods with a credit card rather than cash. A credit card allows you to buy goods on credit without making repayment agreements with the shop.

When someone pays with a credit card, the shop claims the cost of the goods from the company which supplies the card. The credit card company then sends the card holder a statement showing what has been bought and how much money is owed. The credit card holder only has to pay a small percentage of the total amount straight away. But in addition, the credit card holder is charged interest on the sum of money he or she owes the credit card company.

Above: Money and goods change hands several times before a new house is finally paid for. The builder has to borrow money to build the house, and pays interest until the completed house is sold.

Below: The bureau de change shows how much foreign currency they sell for £1, and how much their customers have to pay to get £1 back. The bureau makes a small profit on each transaction because of the difference in the rates for buying and selling.

Bureau de Change

Rates of Exchange per £

9 NOVEMBER 1977

		WE BUY AT		WE SELL AT
		Trav/Cheques	Foreign Notes	Foreign Notes
AUSTRIA		29·30	30·75	28·75
BELGIUM		64·	66·25	63·25
CANADA		2·015	2·05	2·
DENMARK		11·11	11·38	10·98
FRANCE		8·79	9·03	8·71
W.GERMANY		4·10	4·26	4·04
GREECE		65·	72·	69·
HOLLAND		4·40	4·59	4·37
ITALY		1593	1625	1570
NORWAY		9·94	10·21	9·85
PORTUGAL		73·75	77·50	73·50
SPAIN		REFER	155·	150·
SWEDEN		8·70	8·97	8·62
SWITZERLAND		4·04	4·19	3·97
U.S.A		1·83	1·8525	1·8025
JAPAN		452·	475·	450·

These rates do not necessarily apply to notes of large denominations.
Rates for other currencies will be quoted on request
All exchanges are subject to commission charge

Midland Bank

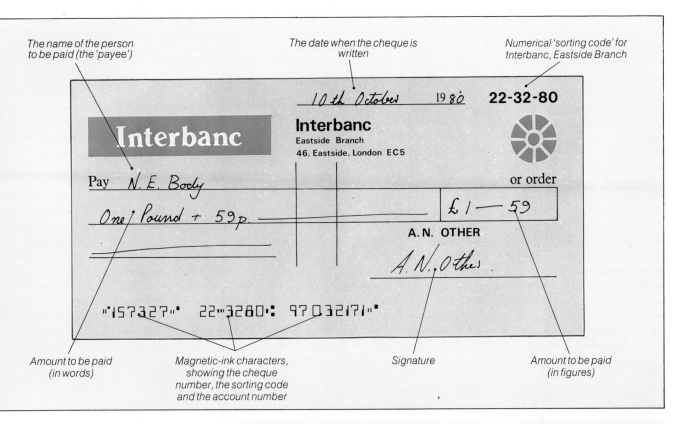

The name of the person to be paid (the 'payee')

The date when the cheque is written

Numerical 'sorting code' for 1interbanc, Eastside Branch

Interbanc

10th October 19 *80* **22-32-80**

Interbanc
Eastside Branch
46, Eastside, London EC5

Pay *N. E. Body*   or order

One Pound + 59p.   £1 — 59

A. N. OTHER

A. N. Other

"157327" 22"3280: 97032171"

Amount to be paid (in words)

Magnetic-ink characters, showing the cheque number, the sorting code and the account number

Signature

Amount to be paid (in figures)

Above: When N.E. Body takes the cheque to the bank, £1.95 is added to his or her account. Body's bank then sends the cheque to Other's bank at Eastside, London, which subtracts £1.95 from Other's account.

Right: The window of this Mexican shop shows the variety of credit cards which it accepts. Using a credit card is a way of borrowing the money. The card company charges interest if the loan if not repaid straight away.

Tax

Nearly everyone who works pays income tax, based on the amount of money they earn. The rate of income tax is expressed as a percentage of taxable income. In the United Kingdom, people pay about 30 per cent income tax on the moneys they earn above the tax-free allowance.

Value added tax (VAT) is also calculated as a percentage. When a firm buys materials from its suppliers, a certain percentage is added to the bill for VAT. The firm then charges its own customers VAT at the same percentage when it sells the finished product to them. A firm usually sells its product at a higher price than it pays for raw materials. So it receives more VAT than it has to pay out, and sends the difference to the government.

New technology

Advanced technology depends on advanced mathematics. Computers were made possible by technological advances, but now it is the computers which are bringing about new advances.

Weather forecasting

In the distant past, forecasters depended on their own observations and experience to predict the weather. But in 1916 a scientist at the British Meteorological Office had the idea that the behaviour of the atmosphere could be described by a series of mathematical equations. Forecasters could use these equations to calculate how the weather would change from hour to hour.

The only problem was that the calculations were so long and complicated that they could not be completed quickly enough to keep up with changes in the weather. Weather forecasters now use powerful computers which can carry out the necessary calculations in a few seconds.

Improving design

Builders, architects and engineers all use computers to help them with their calculations. When building a bridge, the computer calculates the stresses in the structure and makes sure that it is strong enough. It also works out the exact quantities of materials needed to build it. Before an office block is built, a computer can calculate how much energy will be needed to heat the building in winter and keep it cool in summer.

Oil companies use computers to work out the cost of exploring a new oilfield. Once the field is operating, computers monitor and control the flow of oil.

Better than real life

Just as the behaviour of the weather can be imitated by a set of mathematical equations, so almost any system or machine can be represented mathematically. This is called mathematical modelling. Once the equations of the model have been set up, different

Above: The flight deck of a Concorde airliner. The instruments provide the crew with information about the plane's performance and position. Airlines use computerized simulators to train their crew to fly complex new aircraft.

possible designs or actions can be tested out just by putting the right figures into the equations and letting the computer work out the results. For instance, a company that is thinking of opening a new factory in Europe draws up a model with which it tests out different prices, wages, transport costs and other factors. By using mathematical models, planners and engineers can make their mistakes on the computer, rather than having a real-life disaster.

Simulators are an even more realistic way of imitating real life, and are used to train people to operate complicated machines. In an aircraft simulator a set of controls and instruments from the flight deck are linked to the computer. As the pilot operates the controls, the computer makes the instruments behave exactly as they would in a real aircraft. A film projected through the windscreen shows, for example, the approach to a particular airport, while hydraulic rams move the cockpit about to give a realistic 'feel'.

The computer can be programmed to simulate emergencies such as an engine failure or a fire. If the pilot makes a mistake it will even simulate a crash – with the difference that nothing is damaged and the pilot can keep trying until he or she gets it right. Similarly, computer simulation allows training to be given to people who may have to cope with a disaster, such as firemen, ambulance drivers, or engineers in a nuclear power station.

Right: The control room of a giant German chemical works which operates continuously, day and night. Computers help to monitor and control every part of the plant, though human controllers take over in an emergency.

Below: A new office block near San Diego, California. Every aspect of a new development has to be calculated in advance, from the amount of cement required to whether the surrounding roads can cope with the increased traffic it will bring.

Pocket calculators

Electronic calculators are a commonplace mathematical aid. Some are as small and slim as a credit card or fit onto a wrist watch. The main trouble with these tiny machines is that their keys are so small that they cannot be operated easily by an average human finger!

Essential features

Every calculator has three essential features: a power supply, a keyboard and a display. Portable calculators are powered by batteries, but often have built-in transformers which allow them to be plugged into the mains. A few machines have a photo-electric cell which converts sunlight into electricity which is used to recharge the batteries.

Most calculators can display numbers up to eight digits long, though some have ten- or twelve-digit displays. They also have a minus sign for negative numbers and a decimal point which 'floats', i.e. it can appear in any position on the display.

Each digit is built up from seven small straight lines. When all seven are illuminated it makes up the figure '8'; without the centre line it shows '0', and so on. There are two kinds of display: liquid-crystal displays (LCD), and the light-emitting diode (LED) type. LEDs are the older type which glow red or green. LCDs form black figures on a pale background.

The number of keys on a calculator varies, though there are rarely more than 40. At the centre of the keyboard are the nine digits 1,2,3,4,5,6,7,8,9, arranged in an internationally agreed square format. (Incidentally, this is different from the standard format for telephone keyboards, which can be confusing!)

The keys which allow the user to carry out specific mathematical procedures are called function keys. Most calculators also have a key which gives the total for a calculation, sometimes marked with the sign '='. But this is not usually necessary as the total for each stage of the calculation is displayed as the calculation progresses.

Memories

Many calculators have a memory. This is used to store mathematical constants which are needed several times, or the answer to a previous calculation that will be needed again. Simple calculators lose the contents of the memory

Right: The main features of a normal pocket calculator, shown here about twice life size. When choosing a calculator make sure that it has all the features you need, but do not waste money on a complex calculator with features you will never use.

It is important to switch the power off after use to avoid wasting the batteries and possibly damaging the calculator. Some machines have an automatic switch which turns the machine off after a few minutes if it is not being used.

Special function keys provide short cuts for calculations which are used a lot. Specialist calculators have many more special function keys. Scientific calculators have trigonometric, logarithm and exponential functions which do away with the need for mathematical tables.

The clear key C is always used to wipe clear the whole calculator (except the memory) when beginning a new calculation. If a mistake is made while keying in a number, the last number can be cleared and corrected by pressing the CE key, which leaves the rest of the calculation unaffected.

The display usually contains eight digits or more. The glowing LED displays are cheap and can be seen in the dark. Many calculators now have LCD displays which are more economical since they use much less power.

The numeral keys are always arranged in the same format. The positions of the '0' and decimal point keys may vary slightly, though they are usually somewhere below the other nine numeral keys.

Batteries are the most usual source of power, but many calculators can be used with a mains adaptor which converts mains electricity to a suitable low voltage. Some machines have rechargeable batteries which are charged from the mains.

The red keys operate the memory. A number shown on the display can be added to or subtracted from the number in the memory by pressing M+ or M−. The number stored in the memory is displayed by pressing MR, and the contents of the memory are cleared or erased by pressing CM. Many calculators have two or more memories for storing a number of constants.

The simple arithmetic function keys. If the contacts on the keys are badly made they may wear out quickly, leading to mistakes and irritating delays. The slim, credit-card sized calculators have pressure-sensitive keys and emit a bleep to show that a key has been pressed.

when they are switched off, though more sophisticated models will retain the contents of the memory.

As well as the simple, cheap calculators for everyday use, there are many other machines designed for specialists. Some carry special functions needed by scientists, business people or engineers. Computer programmers can buy calculators which will carry out calculations in different number bases.

Some calculators can even take simple programs, and act like tiny computers. The manufacturers have libraries of programs which cope with every type of calculation, from biorhythms to astrology to navigation at sea. There is even a calculator which is specially equipped for working out how much chlorine should be put into swimming pools.

Microprocessors

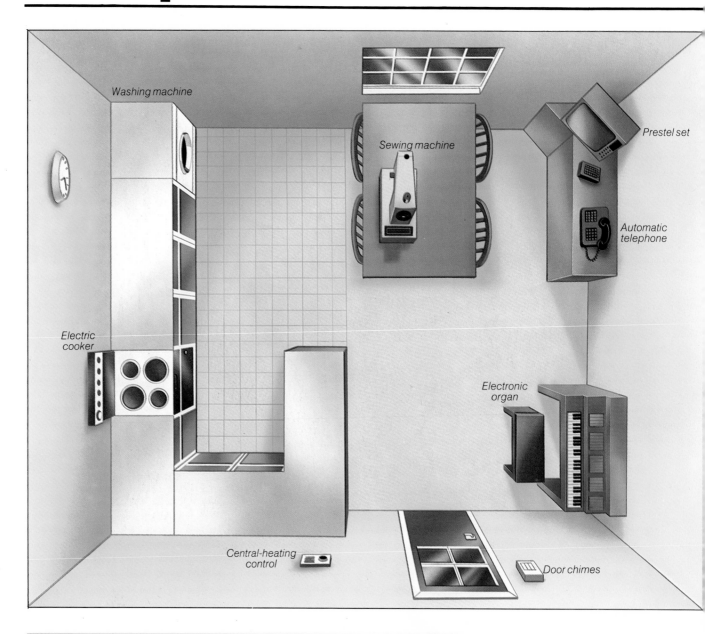

Washing machine

Sewing machine

Prestel set

Electric cooker

Automatic telephone

Electronic organ

Central-heating control

Door chimes

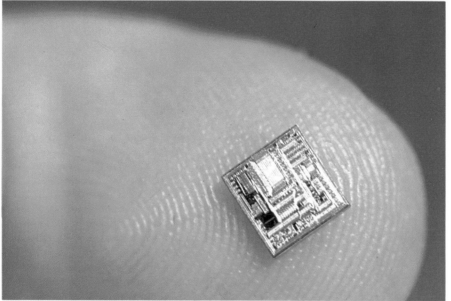

Above: Some of the devices used at home which include microprocessors. Microprocessors are being used in so many appliances because each chip can be sold quite cheaply when mass-produced.

Left: Hundreds of electrical connections are packed into a single microprocessor chip. It is less than 10mm square.

The microprocessor – the 'mighty micro' – is affecting most people's lives in one way or another. This tiny electronic component can contain an enormous processing power. Most importantly, microprocessors can be mass-produced cheaply.

Tiny chips

The silicon chip is the basis of microprocessors. It is a thin piece of pure silicon, less than 10 mm square. Each ilicon slice is coated with a pattern of hemicals which alters the electrical properties of different small areas. These areas are connected together, and to contacts on the edge of the chip, by minute metal paths or circuits which conduct electricity.

The electrical circuits are designed to process the information in the electrical signals which are fed to them. A microprocessor's circuits are set up to perform a particular task. Some 'general purpose' chips can be used in a number of different ways, depending on how their terminals are connected to other components. Some chips are designed for one specialized job only. Most of the cost of making a microprocessor is in setting up the manufacturing process, so it can be very expensive to buy specialized chips which have been made in only small quantities.

Reliability

Microprocessors contain no moving parts, so they are much more reliable than mechanical devices doing the same job. They are also much smaller. Microprocessors are now fitted in many types of machines which used to be purely mechanical. For example, they are commonly used in cash registers, taximeters and petrol pumps, where they accurately record and calculate how much money to charge.

Microprocessors are appearing in many domestic appliances too. Washing machines, cookers, sewing machines, cameras and even door chimes can all be microprocessor controlled. The microprocessor makes it possible for cookers and washing machines to provide a much wider range of automatic operations. The microprocessors in sewing machines are programmed to do embroidery stitches and to sew buttonholes automatically. Some manufacturers supply extra plug-in units containing special programs for elaborate operations.

Micros in industry

The car industry was one of the first to experiment with microprocessors. Most major manufacturers now use 'robots' which are programmed to carry out repetitive tasks on the assembly line. Microprocessors are also built into the cars themselves, where they monitor and control fuel consumption and the emission of

poisonous exhaust gases. There is scope for using microprocessors in all the car's instruments.

Elsewhere in industry, microprocessors are replacing mechanical and electrical machinery. In engineering, they control precision cutting equipment. In the textile industry, microprocessors are being built into weaving looms.

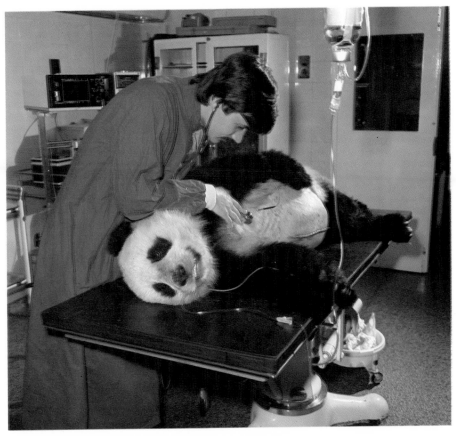

Above: Ching-Ching, London Zoo's giant panda, had to have an operation in 1980. The vet implanted a microprocessor-controlled transmitter in her leg to monitor her progress while she was recovering.

Below: A technician manufacturing microprocessors. Everything is kept perfectly clean as the chips will not work if they become contaminated with dust or unwanted chemicals.

Desk-top computers

Above: Schools are being encouraged to buy their own computers, and computer education in schools and colleges is growing fast. As computers are now used so much in business, engineering and science, it is important that as many people as possible know how to use them before they start work. Electronics and programming are becoming important practical subjects. Schools and colleges also use computers as teaching tools for other subjects. Mathematics students use computers to solve problems, while geography and science students use them to analyse statistics. As new software is developed, computers can help to teach almost any subject in new and more interesting ways. Schools can also use their computers in administrative tasks, such as working out a new timetable, or planning lunch rotas.

The big computers of the 1950s and 1960s needed dozens of people to operate them. They were costly to buy and had to be housed in special air-conditioned rooms. Nowadays the cost of one person's wages for a few weeks buys a powerful computer which can be plugged into the mains, ready to go. These microcomputers, designed to be used in ordinary office conditions, are making themselves felt in business, in teaching and at home.

This has made microcomputers one of the fastest growing areas of the computer industry. During the late 1970s, dozens of manufacturers began to produce their own machines. At the same time, a bewildering variety of printers, disc drives and other peripheral units also became available.

Micro and Mini

Microcomputers are usually built around one or more microprocessor chips, and probably contain a number of RAM chips too. The simplest models do not even need any computer peripherals. They can use an ordinary cassette recorder and cassette tape to store and enter information, and a television set instead of a VDU to display information. They have been sold as personal computers to people who are interested in computing as a hobby.

Small businesses, which had not been able to afford a large computer, soon realised that a microcomputer could be very useful to help them keep control over their operations and accounts. The manufacturers responded by bringing out microcomputers designed especially for businesses. The biggest of these are so powerful that they have earned the name 'minicomputers'.

Software packages

Business people wanted to use computers, but they did not have the experience to write their own programs. So the suppliers have developed sets of programs which people can buy and

On the farm

Right: There are plenty of jobs for the microcomputer down on the farm. Dairy farmers always keep records to show how much milk is produced by each cow in their herd. A computer records each animal's yield. By showing how the milk yield is changing from day to day the computer can help the farmer to judge the best type of feed to use, and whether other changes need to be made to the herd. It can also be used for general accounts, calculating wages and other business purposes.

se for general business applications, uch as accounting. These sets of standard programs are sometimes called software packages'. Almost every onceivable activity is catered for. here are software packages for uilders, dentists and doctors, news-agents, hotels, chemists, petrol stations, lawyers, vets, shops and antique dealers, to mention just a few.

Many people find that computing makes a fascinating hobby. They buy microcomputers to use in their spare time. They teach themselves to program, and use their machines to work out household expenses, keep diaries and shopping lists, plan menus for parties – and to play games, of course. You can even buy a micro-computer in kit form and build it yourself.

The dentist's surgery

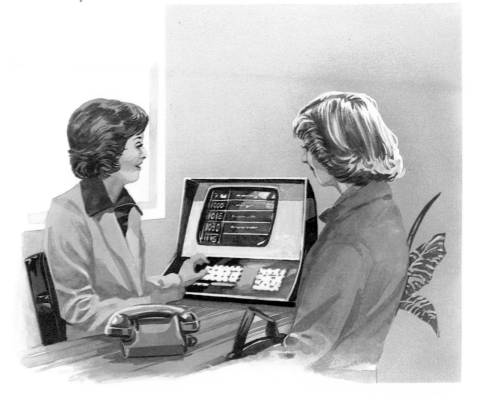

Above: Special programs have been developed to help dentists run their surgeries more efficiently. A computer can be used to store and display the charts which show the condition of each patient's teeth, and to record the treatment which they have received. The receptionist uses it to keep the diary of appointments and to calculate their fees for treatment. It can even be programmed to send out a reminder to each patient to make an appointment for a check-up.

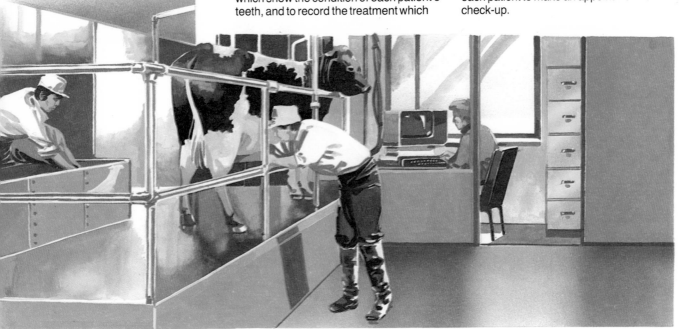

Computer games

Computers are good at following rules – in fact they can do nothing else – so a computer can play any game from roulette to chess. For many years, programmers have tackled the challenge of devising a program to play chess as well as a human Grand Master. But the most popular games are completely new ones which rely on the computer's ability to display complicated, fast-moving graphics on a screen.

TV games

Television games or 'video games' plug into ordinary television sets. The control units contain a microprocessor which is designed solely to play the game. The program, containing all the instructions to the computer, comes on a ROM which is usually built in. Some units can be used to play a variety of different games by slotting in the appropriate ROM.

The big computer games machines that are installed in cafes and amusement arcades are just as popular. As with the TV games, it is possible to select different levels of play. Some machines are programmed to become more difficult to beat as the player becomes more skilful. These machines have very large memories, dedicated to playing just one game. This means that they can produce a better quality picture on the screen, with more spectacular sound effects, and include more variation of speed and skill. Altogether, they can be made more exciting than the smaller TV games.

Computer toys

Some manufacturers are now making portable, computerized toys. Most units consists of a small display and a set of buttons – rather like an overgrown calculator. Like the TV games, the programs are supplied on a ROM which is slotted into the unit.

Many of these toys have an educational purpose too. Some have mathematical problems stored in the memory, others test the player's ability to spell difficult words. The player picks problems at random. When the player answers, by pressing the appropriate keys, the machine indicates whether the answer is right or wrong.

Sophisticated versions of these toys have been turned into portable dictionaries for foreign words and

phrases. Travellers enter the word they need in their own language. From the list of words in its ROM, the computer chooses the corresponding foreign word.

Living history

Some of the most fascinating and challenging computer games are based on simulations of real-life events, past or future. History students can simulate important historical events such as the French Revolution or the American War of Independence. The computer runs through events as they took place, giving the student the opportunity of deciding what they would have done if they had been there at the time. The computer then alters events to take their decisions into account.

Left: Various versions of *Space Invaders* made video games popular for the first time. Coin-in-the slot machines appeared all over the world in cafes, bars and bus stations. Special sound effects add to the excitement of these games.

Above: Chess computers like the *Chess Challenger* play the game against human opponents. They can be adjusted to play at any standard, from beginner up. Some models will even give a Grand Master a good match.

Below: Playing a TV game at home can be an amusing alternative to watching the programmes. You play against the computer or against another player. Many models have plug-in memory modules to provide a variety of different games.

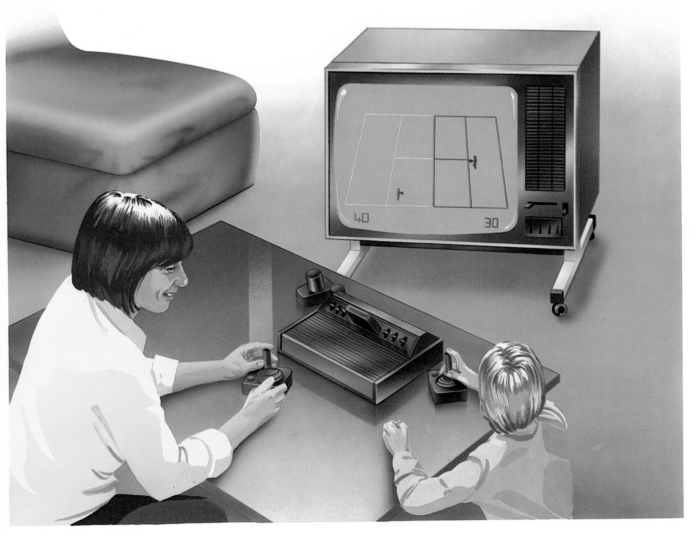

Spanning the globe

Above: The control room at Houston, Texas which guided the American Apollo missions to the moon. The journey would have been impossible without the computers on the ground and in the space vehicles. The astronauts were trained on computer simulators.

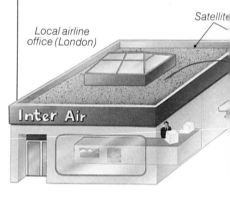

Computers, large and small, are used in offices and factories, schools and hospitals, building sites and oil rigs. They store, sort and process information for human beings to use. A single computer is powerful enough for simple tasks, but for large data-bases more complicated interconnected systems are needed. These may include hundreds of peripheral units spread round an office – or even round the world. Some of these may be 'intelligent' terminals containing limited data-processing power to share some of the work with the central processor.

Police work
Most police forces find plenty of work for their computer systems. They monitor emergency calls for help to ensure a fast response. In large cities,

computers control traffic lights to help the traffic flow.

The details of everyone who has been convicted of a crime are stored in police computers, including information about their fingerprints. This helps the police keep track of known criminals, and can often be used in solving new crimes.

The enormous amount of information which can be stored and then quickly retrieved again worries people who believe that the police or the government may sometimes exceed their proper powers. A detailed picture of any citizen's life can be pieced together from the information about their tax, their work, their car and so on, which is stored in the various computers. This gives a great deal of power to the people who actually control the computers. Many countries have passed laws to ensure that computers are not used to invade people's privacy.

Word processing
A word processor is a computer system which is designed to store and process written text. Once it has been entered

into the system, the text can be called up onto a VDU and edited: the user can change, add or delete words. Spelling mistakes can be corrected, or whole paragraphs can be changed. If the text is needed in printed form it can be fed to a printer, or it is stored away again until required. The word processor will also arrange the text into columns or pages. This makes it useful for preparing text that is going to be made into a book, magazine or newspaper.

Word processing is already being used in hundreds of offices. Where a similar letter is being sent out to several different people the letter need only be typed once. The names, addresses and details for each person are then fed in, and the machine types an individual letter for each of them.

Word processors are useful for preparing documents which have to be rewritten several times before they are complete. For example, lawyers often alter legal documents several times before they are sent out. Instead of typing them out in full each time, the typist just taps in the corrections and the machine does the rest.

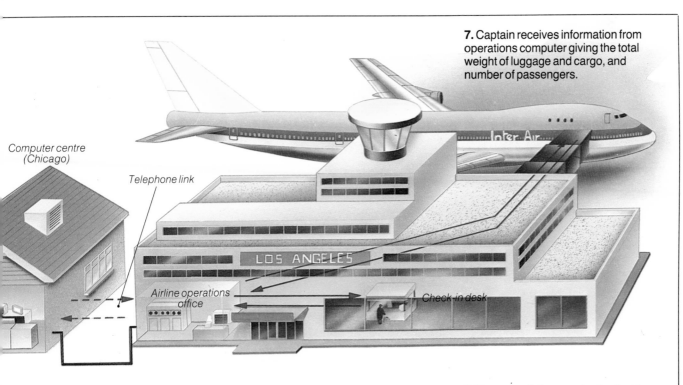

7. Captain receives information from operations computer giving the total weight of luggage and cargo, and number of passengers.

Computer centre (Chicago)

Telephone link

Airline operations office

Check-in desk

LOS ANGELES

4. The passenger arrives at Los Angeles check-in. The desk clerk enters the name and flight details into VDU terminal and checks with information from central computer.

5. Computer confirms that passenger is booked on flight.

6. Passenger's luggage is checked in and weighed. Details are entered on VDU and stored locally.

Above: Airline offices are linked to the airline's central computer. At the airport, the desk clerk checks the passenger's booking in the central computer. The local computer stores details of the aircraft's load to be relayed to the captain.

Right: Computers of any size can be linked to a suitable printer to form a word-processing system. Word processors can even be connected to phototypesetters which set text ready for printing.

Airlines

Computers are used extensively in aviation. Pilots are trained on computer simulators, and the cockpit of an aircraft is packed with computerized instruments. On the ground, airlines have massive computer installations which can tell them at a moment's notice where a particular plane is, who is piloting it, and how much fuel it is carrying. The airlines have set up an international computer network which allows airline representatives or travel agents anywhere in the world to know instantly if there is a vacant seat on a certain flight.

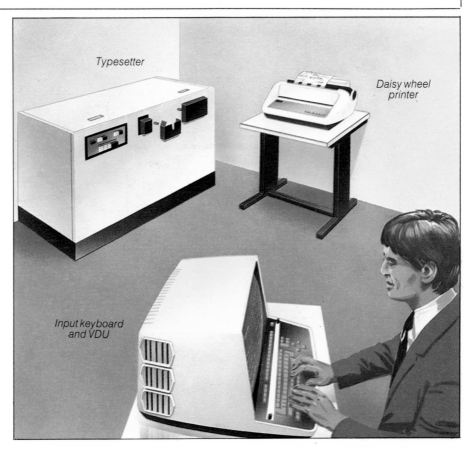

Typesetter

Daisy wheel printer

Input keyboard and VDU

The world tomorrow

Coming soon...

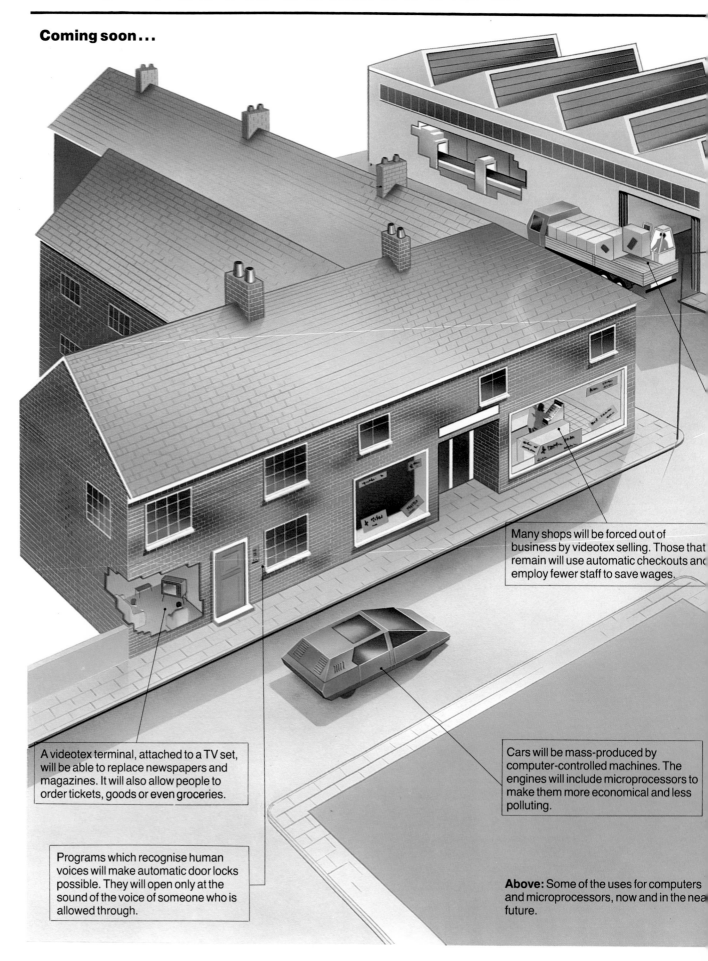

Many shops will be forced out of business by videotex selling. Those that remain will use automatic checkouts and employ fewer staff to save wages.

A videotex terminal, attached to a TV set, will be able to replace newspapers and magazines. It will also allow people to order tickets, goods or even groceries.

Cars will be mass-produced by computer-controlled machines. The engines will include microprocessors to make them more economical and less polluting.

Programs which recognise human voices will make automatic door locks possible. They will open only at the sound of the voice of someone who is allowed through.

Above: Some of the uses for computers and microprocessors, now and in the near future.

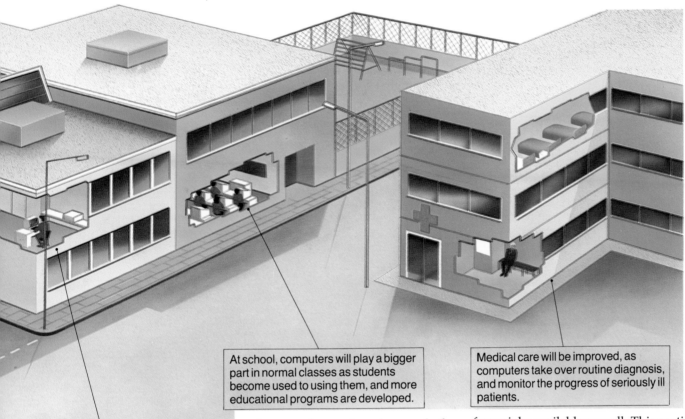

At school, computers will play a bigger part in normal classes as students become used to using them, and more educational programs are developed.

Medical care will be improved, as computers take over routine diagnosis, and monitor the progress of seriously ill patients.

In offices, most paperwork will be replaced by electronic communication through computer terminals. Some people will be able to work through a computer terminal in their home instead of travelling to work every day.

On factory production lines, electronically controlled robots will replace many human workers.

Computers are more efficient than people at doing many jobs. For this reason, computers and computer-controlled devices will take over a large number of jobs which used to be carried out by human beings.

New jobs
This will bring many advantages with it. Computer-controlled machines will be able to perform jobs that are too dangerous for human beings to do. They will also do jobs that are very dull and repetitive, that human beings do not want to do.

But in addition to taking over dangerous and repetitive work, computers will also replace human beings doing skilled work. For example, computers are being used more

and more in engineering and the manufacture of precision instruments. They are doing jobs that gave people good wages and satisfaction, and for which they spent several years learning their trade. These trained people will no longer be able to use their hard-earned skills.

New problems
The printing industry is a good example of how computerization may affect all of industry. The process of getting a writer's work into print is a long one which involves many skilled crafts. The introduction of computerized methods for typesetting and plate making means that many of these skills will not be needed. The printers are very unhappy about the prospect of being thrown out of work by computers. Through their unions they are refusing to allow computerization unless they are also assured that they will not all lose their jobs.

Many people have started their working life in an office, doing typing or filing and other administrative tasks. Word processors, which store and print documents, are already taking the place of office clerks and typists. Although people will be required to operate the word processors and other computers in the office, there will be

fewer jobs available overall. This particularly affects women, who have traditionally worked in offices as typists and filing clerks.

Computers will create some new jobs. In particular, people will be needed to develop new computers and write programs for new applications. In offices and factories, people will be needed to operate computers and computer controlled machines. However, not everyone wants to change to a job which forces them to sit in front of a flashing VDU all day.

Leisure or unemployment?
There is no doubt that computers will make many aspects of life much easier. Computers should mean better medical care, better education, more efficient government and more profitable businesses.

Fewer people will be needed to do the work now being done by the whole workforce. What will happen as a result?

Many people could be forced into unemployment and idleness, while just a few have interesting, well-paid jobs. Alternatively, the benefits of computers could be shared, with good pay, long holidays and plenty of leisure time for everyone. These are some problems which must be solved.

A-Z glossary

Abacus A simple device which is used as an aid in arithmetic calculations. A series of rods or wires is mounted in a frame, with a number of beads strung on each wire. Although it is simple and cheap, skilled users can work faster with an abacus than with an electronic calculator.

Algol A computer language used mainly by mathematicians.

Analog computer A machine which calculates by altering the size of various electrical signals within it. Analog computers were built for special scientific purposes, but most of the jobs they were used for can be done faster by modern digital machines.

ASCII The abbreviation for American Standard Code for Information Interchange. It was adopted in 1963 by the American National Standards Institute, as a standard for the coding of information into binary.

Bar code A row of dark and light stripes forming a characteristic pattern. When scanned by a laser it produces a signal which can be recognised by a computer. Bar codes are being introduced on supermarket goods, and allow automation of both checkouts and stock control.

A bar code

Base (1) The number of digits used in a number system. Our usual number system is base-ten. (2) The number on which a logarithm is based.

Base ten A number system which uses ten symbols to construct numbers, and counts by multiples of ten; a decimal system.

Basic A general-purpose computer language used on most modern, small computers. Each manufacturer uses a slightly different form of Basic in their system software, so programs designed for one make of machine may not run on another type.

Bit An abbreviation for **bi**nary dig**it**.

Byte The unit used to describe the size of a computer's memory. One byte is the string of binary digits which represents a single letter, numeral or other character.

Cobol A computer language suitable for business use.

CPU Central processing unit; the part of a computer that actually processes information by sorting and analysing it.

Cube The product of raising a number to the power of 3; the product of multiplying a number by itself, and then multiplying the answer by the original number.

Data Information which has not been processed. The raw material with which the computer works.

Data base A body of related information which can be reached through a computer system.

Decimal Number system based on ten; derived from the Latin word *decem* which means 'ten'.

Digit A single symbol in a number system. The decimal system has ten digits: 1,2,3,4,5, 6,7,8,9,0. The binary system has only two: 1,0.

Digital computer A computer that functions by processing information in the form of electronic signals which represent binary digits. All present-day electronic computers are digital computers.

Direct data entry Entering data straight into a computer system through a VDU or other keyboard, rather than through an intermediate medium such as a card, tape or disc.

Disc A device for storing data. As on a tape recorder, information is stored on a thin magnetic film on the surface of the disc. The disc spins rapidly, while a head which reads or records the information can be moved in towards the centre of the disc or away from it. Information from any position on the disc can therefore be recalled more quickly than from a tape – which has to be wound on to the correct position – but not as quickly as from a RAM.

EBDIC The abbreviation for Extended Binary Coded Decimal Interchange Code. Along with ASCII it is a standard for coding information into binary.

Floppy disc A cheap form of magnetic disc. It cannot store as much information as a rigid disc, and wears out more quickly.

Flow chart A diagram which shows all the actions and decisions required to reach a particular goal. Programmers use flow charts to break down problems into their basic units before writing detailed programs.

Fortran A computer language used mainly for scientific programming.

Hardware The electronic machinery which makes up a computer system.

Information The output from a computer, arranged in a form which has meaning, and which can be understood.

Integer A whole number.

Intelligent An intelligent terminal is one which has some data-processing power of its own, and can do some operations independently of the central computer.

Interest The money paid by someone who borrows money to the person who has lent it. Interest is usually expressed as a percentage of the loan to be paid each month or year. The loan itself also has to be paid back eventually, as well as the interest.

Irrational number A number which cannot be expressed in the form of a fraction; π and e are irrational numbers.

Kilobyte One thousand bytes (abbreviated as 1 kb).

Logarithm If $a = 10^n$, then n is said to be the logarithm of a (to the base 10).
The logarithm of 10 is 1 – since $10 = 10^1$; the logarithm of 100 is 2 – since $100 = 10^2$; the logarithm of 1000 is 3.
The logarithm of the product of two numbers multiplied together is equal to the sum of their individual logarithms: $\log(a \times b) = \log a + \log b$.

Logarithmic scale A scale on which length is proportional to the logarithm of each number. It is used when proportion is more important than absolute size: pairs of numbers of equal proportion are always the same distance apart on a logarithmic scale.

Magnetic ink character recognition (MICR) A system by which a computer can read specially formed characters printed in magnetic ink. The reader scans each symbol vertically in several places and detects how much of the space is covered in ink. If more than half is inked it generates a binary 1; if less than half it generates a 0. In this way a string of bits is generated for each symbol.

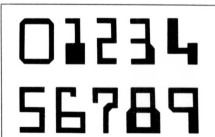

Magnetic-ink characters

Mainframe A very large, powerful computer, which usually consists of a number of separate units and needs clean air and cool temperatures to work properly.

Mathematical model A set of mathematical equations which describes a complicated process or system. The behaviour of the system can be studied by looking at the changes which take place when different conditions are fed into the system. Mathematical models are used in setting up simulators.

Megabyte One million bytes (abbreviated as 1 MB).

Microcomputer A small, self-contained computer.

Microprocessor A processing unit based on a silicon chip. Most small computers contain several microprocessors doing different tasks.

Minicomputer A medium-sized computer.

Naperian logarithms (Also called natural logarithms.) Logarithms which are based on powers at a number called e, which is approximately equal to 2·7. This seemingly curious number crops up in a number of important equations in mathematics and physics.

Optical character recognition (OCR) A system by which a computer can 'read' typed or printed material. Most OCR systems require specially formed characters, which can be read by eye as well as by the computer.

Optical mark recognition A system in which a computer detects the presence or absence of a mark on a piece of paper at a particular position.

Peripheral Any part of a computer, other than the CPU. Peripherals of various kinds are used for entering data, storing it and gathering information out of the machine.

Power A number is raised to the nth power when it is multiplied by itself n times. For example 2 raised to the power of 4 ($= 2 \times 2 \times 2 \times 2$) = 16. It can be written 2^4.

Prestel The trade name for the videotex service provided by British Telecom.

Prime number A number which when divided by any other number (apart from 1) does not give a whole number, i.e. it can only be divided by itself and 1.

Program A set of instructions which tells the computer what to do.

Random access memory (RAM) A memory unit which can be used over and over again (like magnetic tape) and from which any piece of information can be read very quickly.

Random sample A selection of things or information which have been chosen from a larger group by chance; a random sample should therefore be typical of the larger group.

Rational number A number which can be expressed in the form of a fraction.

Read only memory (ROM) A memory unit from which information cannot be erased. ROMs are used for storing vital instruction programs.

Read-write head A device which records and reads data on a magnetic tape or disc. On magnetic tape and floppy discs the head comes into contact with the surface. On hard discs it flies across the surface without touching, and this means that a tiny particle of dust can cause the head to crash onto the disc surface and damage the data stored on it.

Root The inverse of a power. If $a = b^n$ (a is

the nth power of b) then b is said to be the nth root of a.

Silicon chip A tiny slice of pure silicon, which is chemically treated and engraved with minute electrical circuits. When complete it acts in the same way as an assembly of hundreds of individual electronic components. Many kinds of chips are made to act as processors (microprocessors) or memory units.

Simulator A machine, usually controlled by a computer, which imitates the behaviour of complex systems and allows people to learn how to control complex machines in safety.

Software Another name for computer programs. The programs which instruct the CPU on how to run itself and its peripherals are called system software. Additional programs to solve particular problems are called application software.

Square The product of a number multiplied by itself; the result of raising a number to the power of 2. Square numbers are the squares of integers.

Square root The square root of a number, when multiplied by itself, gives the number first thought of. For example 3 is the square root of 9. This is written: $3 = \sqrt{9}$ (since $3 \times 3 = 9$).

Statistics Numerical information about a particular subject.

Terminal A peripheral unit such as a VDU or a printer for entering data and displaying information. Terminals are usually separate

from the main computer, and may be sited many miles away and linked to the computer by a telephone line.

Timesharing A computer works so fast that it can be used by a number of different operators at the same time. In fact at any moment, the computer is available to only one of the operators, but it switches from one to another so quickly that each operator seems to have the computer's undivided attention. It is called timesharing because the CPU is dividing up its time between the many operators.

Vector A quantity which has both size and direction, such as force, speed, movement etc.

Videotex A computer system which allows subscribers to have access to information from an extremely large data-base. The information is displayed on a specially adapted television set which is connected into the system through ordinary telephone lines. The subscriber is charged for the information used, though some information such as advertising is provided free.

Visual display unit (VDU) A screen, similar to a television screen, used to display information from a computer and controlled by a keyboard.

Word processor A computer system which stores text and allows it to be called up on a VDU to be changed and edited, before being typed out as hard copy or set in type for printing.

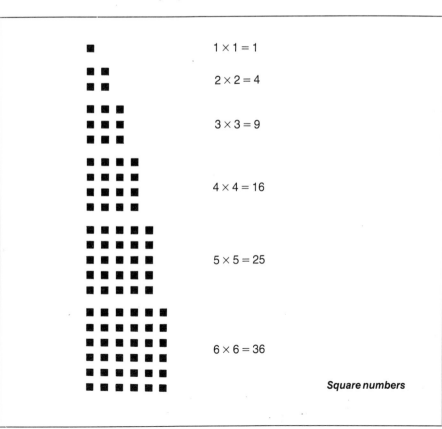

Square numbers

$1 \times 1 = 1$

$2 \times 2 = 4$

$3 \times 3 = 9$

$4 \times 4 = 16$

$5 \times 5 = 25$

$6 \times 6 = 36$

Reference

People and dates

The chronology below lists just a few of the significant developments which have led to the powerful digital computers of today.

1617 John Napier, the inventor of logarithms, announced the invention of his 'bones', which were a series of numbered rods designed for doing multiplication and division. They were one of the first ways of doing calculations with the help of a mechanical device.

1642 The world's first digital calculator was built by a Frenchman, Blaise Pascal. It consisted of a series of numbered wheels connected together by gears and chains. Numbers were entered into the machine by dialling them in on the wheels. The machine could 'carry' to the next wheel on the left when necessary.

1694 The German mathematician Gottfried Leibnitz invented an improved calculating machine called the 'stepped reckoner'. As well as adding, it could multiply, divide and work out square roots by the process of repeated addition. Modern digital computers work on the same principle.

1801 Joseph Jaquard, a French engineer, designed a silk loom controlled by an endless belt of punched cards. The cards were 'read' by jets of compressed air. These in turn operated the machinery controlling the coloured threads in the warp of the cloth.

1835 Charles Babbage completed his designs for an 'analytical engine'. This could not only do complex calculations, but could also be programmed so that the machine itself decided which branch of a program to take, depending on the results of earlier calculations. Both data and programs were to be fed into the machine on punched cards.

1946 ENIAC was completed at the University of Pennsylvania. It used 150 kW of electrical power, and was estimated to be over 1000 times faster than the most advanced electro-mechanical machine, the Harvard Mark I, completed in 1944.

1947 EDVAC (Electronic Discrete Variable Automatic Computer), was completed. EDVAC was the first computer with an electronic memory for storing data and programs.

1951 UNIVAC 1 was built for the United States Bureau of Census. This was the first time a computer was put to practical use sorting information, rather than simply doing long calculations.

1955 The magnetic core store was developed to replace memory circuits using electronic (thermionic) valves. The core stores worked much more rapidly than the memories they replaced, greatly increasing the speed of information processing. They also used much less power.

1957 The second generation of computers, using transistors instead of valves, came into service. Transistors were much more compact than the valves which they replaced, allowing more processing power to be packed into a small space. They also used much less electrical power, so it was easier to cool the circuits of the newer machines.

c. 1967 The third generation of computers were introduced, using integrated circuits instead of separate electronic components.
They were still more compact and faster than second generation machines.

1971 The first microprocessor was introduced in which a single integrated circuit contained all the components of a processing unit. Microprocessors led the way to cheap microcomputers and are being developed for use in ultra-fast computers for the 1980s. Direct input keyboards and other input devices allow computer operators to enter instructions and data using the ordinary numbers and letters of the alphabet. System software within the computer automatically transforms each character into a string of binary digits which can then be processed.

Books to read

There are literally thousands of books available about mathematics, many of which are straightforward textbooks of the kind which everyone has met at school. But in addition there are a number of books which highlight the more curious and interesting facets of mathematics.

Mathematicians's Delight by W.W. Sawyer, published by William Gannon, sets out to dispel its readers' fear of the subject. It includes sections on geometry, logic, algebra — the mathematical shorthand — graphs and calculus. In a similar vein, *Riddles in Mathematics* by Eugene P. Northrop describes a number of entertaining paradoxes in various branches of mathematics. The ideas of modern mathematics, including sets, number and topology, are presented in an equally light-hearted and easily understood manner in *Concepts of Modern Mathematics* by Ian Stewart, published by Oxford University Press.

Mathematics for the Million by Lancelot Hogben, published by W.W. Norton, first appeared in 1936 and has since become something of a classic. It covers the history of mathematics over the last 7000 years as well as the fundamental concepts of number, algebra, geometry and calculus, and links mathematical developments with the mainstream of social and economic history.

By contrast to mathematics, which stretches back throughout recorded history, computers are one of the newest branches of technology. In an area which is changing as fast as the technology of computers, books soon become out of date. However, here is a list of some very helpful books written for young people.

Discovering Computers by Mark Frank Stonehenge Press, 1981
Computers in Your Life by Melvin Berger (Harper and Row, 1978)
Exploring with Computers by Gary G. Bitter (Julian Messner, 1981)
Computers by Richard W. Brown (Viking Press, 1976)
The Human Side of Computers by Daniel Cohen (McGraw-Hill, 1975)
The Calculator Game Book by Arlene Hartman (New American Library, 1977)
Computers for Kids: Atari Edition by Sally G. Larsen (Creative Computing, 1981)
Computers for Kids: Apple II Plus Edition by Sally G. Larsen (Creative Computing, 1981)
Computers for Kids: TRS 80 Edition by Sally G. Larsen (Creative Computing, 1980)
The Story of Computers by Charles T. Meadow (Harvey House, 1970)
Computers in Action: How Computers Work by Donald Spencer (Hayden Book Company, 1978)
What Computers Can Do by Donald Spencer (Camelot Publishing Co., 1977)
Computer Coin Games by Joe Weisbecker (Creative Computing, 1979)
Learning Disk BASIC and DOS by David A. Lien (CompuSoft Publishing, 1982)

Facts and feats

★ In the 18th century, an English mathematician called Charles Babbage worked out the principle of the digital computer. He was unable to put his ideas into practice because of the limitations of the technology of his time.

★ Computers are used to control stage lighting. A microprocessor is programmed to switch the lights on and off, dim them, and change colours as required.

★ It took so long to count and record the

United States population census in 1880 that the government decided to count the next census, ten years later, with the help of electrical machinery. The machines which were chosen used punched cards. The company that supplied them went on to become the largest manufacturer of computers in the world, International Business Machines, IBM.

★ The first mechanical calculator went on sale in 17th century France. At that time, the word 'calculator' meant a person who carried out mathematical calculations, such as working out multiplication tables.

★ It took experts five years to convert the British police force's 2½ million fingerprint records to a form in which they could be stored on a computer.

★ In a microprocessor, all electronic activity takes place on the surface of the chip. The active layer is thinner than the shell of a soap bubble.

★ In the 1979 Tour de France bicycle race, the scores were kept by a computer which travelled around behind the race in the back of a truck.

★ The slide rule was invented by an English country rector in 1621. It was little used outside Britain until the 19th century. Customs officers had special slide rules to help them calculate the tax to be paid on partly-filled barrels of wine and spirits.

★ The Incas kept numerical records by tying knots in lengths of string, since they had no written language. They used the decimal system.

★ The number of beads on a Russian abacus is based on the Russian currency system.

★ During the Second World War the British intelligence service used a computer to decipher enemy codes. This computer, named COLOSSUS, was kept a secret for over 30 years.

★ Less than five out of every 100 silicon chips manufactured are good enough to use, the rest have to be thrown away.

★ The first word processor was developed by the United States Army to produce letters notifying a soldier's family of his death.

★ The keys on a typewriter are arranged to slow typists down! When the mechanical typewriter was first invented, typists could type faster than the typewriter mechanism could move, so all the keys jammed together. The problem does not exist with electronic typewriters, so new keyboard designs are now starting to appear.

Acknowledgements

Artists
Industrial Art Studios and Bob Harvey (represented by David Lewis Artists)

Photographs

Key: T (top); B (bottom); C (centre)

Asahi Pentax: 9T
BPC Picture Library: 16, 26-27, 28
Paul Brierley: front cover, 2-3, 20, 21, 23
British Telecom: 22
Computer Games Limited/Tilbury Sandford Brysson: 39
Daily Telegraph Colour Library: 30, 31B
Ferranti Limited/Rowlinson Broughton: 34
Ford of Britain: 9C
Greater London Council: 13
Key Markets Limited: 19
William Macquitty: 7
Photri: 29, 40
Plessey Semiconductors/Roles and Parker Limited: 35B
Shell U.K.: 25
John Topham Picture Library: 9B
Zefa Picture Library: 11, 31T, 38
Zoological Society of London: 35T

ASCII codes

A	100 0001	X	101 1000	?	011 1111
B	100 0010	Y	101 1001	[	101 1011
C	100 0011	Z	101 1010	\	101 1100
D	100 0100			]	101 1101
E	100 0101			↑	101 1110
F	100 0110	1	011 0001	←	101 1111
G	100 0111	2	011 0010	space	010 0000
H	100 1000	3	011 0011	!	010 0001
I	100 1001	4	011 0100	"	010 0010
J	100 1010	5	011 0101	#	010 0011
K	100 1011	6	011 0110	$	010 0100
L	100 1100	7	011 0111	%	010 0101
M	100 1101	8	011 1000	&	010 0110
N	100 1110	9	011 1001	'	010 0111
O	100 1111	0	011 0000	(	010 1000
P	101 0000			)	010 1001
Q	101 0001			*	010 1010
R	101 0010			+	010 1011
S	101 0011	:	011 1010	,	010 1100
T	101 0100	;	011 1011	—	010 1101
U	101 0101	<	011 1100	.	010 1110
V	101 0110	=	011 1101	/	010 1111
W	101 0111	>	011 1110	@	100 0000

Direct input keyboards and other input devices allow computer operators to enter instructions and data using the ordinary numbers and letters of the alphabet. System software within the computer automatically transforms each character into a string of binary digits which can then be processed.

The ASCII codes were established as a standard for all manufacturers, so that pieces of equipment from different manufacturers could be used together, i.e. they are 'compatible' with each other. As well as the basic alphabet and numerals, the ASCII character set includes a number of special characters which are used for programming or for simple descriptions and text.

Each character is represented by a set of eight bits. Seven of them, shown here, carry the information while the eighth is an extra check digit, usually called a parity bit. If one digit has been altered accidentally, the computer will recognise from the parity bit that something is wrong, and reject the faulty information.

Index